DIRECTIONS IN AMERICAN

Works from
the Collection of
Dr. and Mrs. John J. McDonough

Oswaldo Rodriguez Roque

To Roger Marks with
warm regards and
very best wishes.
John McDonough

Thought you might
enjoy some of the pictures

Say hello to your
lovely wife.

Museum of Art, Carnegie Institute, Pittsburgh

Published in conjunction with the exhibition *Directions in American Painting 1875–1925: Works from the Collection of Dr. and Mrs. John J. McDonough*

Museum of Art, Carnegie Institute, Pittsburgh
June 5–August 8, 1982

Columbus Museum of Art, Columbus, Ohio
October 16–November 28, 1982

Hunter Museum of Art, Chattanooga, Tennessee
January 9–February 27, 1983

Cummer Gallery of Art, Jacksonville, Florida
March 25–May 15, 1983

The exhibition program of the Museum of Art, Carnegie Institute, is supported by grants from the Pennsylvania Council on the Arts and the Howard Heinz Endowment.

Designed by Frank Garrity Graphic Design
Composition by DowntownType
Printed in the United States by Stephenson, Inc.

Library of Congress Cataloging in Publication Data

Rodriguez Roque, Oswaldo, 1949-
Directions in American painting, 1875-1925.

Catalogue of an exhibition organized by the Museum of Art, Carnegie Institute.
Bibliography: p.
1. Painting, American – Exhibitions. 2. Painting, Modern – 19th century – United States – Exhibitions. 3. Painting, Modern – 20th century – United States – Exhibitions. 4. McDonough, John J. – Art collections – Exhibitions. I. Carnegie Institute. Museum of Art. II. Title.
ND210.R6 759.13'074'014886 82-6473
ISBN 0-88039-003-4 AACR2

Cover
Childe Hassam
Gloucester Harbor

Foreword

John J. McDonough has had a lifelong interest in paintings, an interest that had its origin in his first visit as a schoolboy to the Toledo Museum of Art and was further stimulated during his medical student days by the great Impressionist collections of the Art Institute of Chicago.

In 1965 he began to make a collection of American paintings that spanned a two-hundred-year period from the eighteenth century to World War II. In 1975-76 sixty paintings from this collection were in an exhibition organized by the New Orleans Museum of Art and shown there and at museums in San Diego, San Antonio, Little Rock, Greensburg, Raleigh, Oklahoma City, and Youngstown. In 1978 this McDonough Collection was sold in a one-collection auction at Sotheby Park-Bernet, New York, an event of exceptional interest to everyone following the fine American paintings market.

It was not surprising to all who knew Dr. McDonough that, not long after the disposition of his first collection, he found himself unable to resist the urge to start another. However, in the late 1970s when he began to collect again, conditions in the American paintings market had changed dramatically and the prevailing state was and remains one of high and continually increasing prices with a relative scarcity of works of high quality. It is a particular testament to Dr. McDonough's discriminating taste and determination that he has been so successful in forming a second collection that adheres to the same high standards of quality he set for himself in making his first. And, it might be added, in narrowing the focus to a fifty-year period between 1875 and 1925, this new collection has been created with even greater coherence.

Youngstown, Dr. McDonough's home, is closely related to Pittsburgh by geographic proximity and common steel industry traditions. He has been a good friend to all three art museums with significant American collections in the western Pennsylvania-eastern Ohio region: the Museum of Art, Carnegie Institute in Pittsburgh, the Butler Institute of American Art in Youngstown, and the Westmoreland County Museum of Art in Greensburg. And, for the past two decades, he has set the leading example for collecting important American paintings in this part of the nation. The Museum of Art, Carnegie Institute is privileged to have had the opportunity to organize and show the exhibition *Directions in American Painting 1875-1925: Works from the Collection of Dr. and Mrs. John J. McDonough.*

It is a pleasure to acknowledge the generous assistance of the many friends and colleagues who came to our aid in conceiving this exhibition, in mounting it, and in researching its catalogue. First and foremost, thanks are due to Carole and John McDonough for their willingness to part with their collection for a period of over a year. At all times the McDonoughs have proved helpful, encouraging, and patient. It is hoped that the pleasure of seeing their paintings hanging on the walls of the participating four museums will compensate them for having to look at empty ones at home. Furthermore, their promised gift of *Girl in Lavender, Seated at Desk* by Theodore Earl Butler to the Museum of Art, Carnegie Institute on the occasion of the opening of this exhibition is exceptionally generous and will make an important addition to the museum's own highly significant collection of American paintings.

We are grateful to Paul Chew, Director of the Westmoreland County Museum of Art, for his gracious and important advocacy of this project from its outset. We thank, too, our sister institutions that are participating in the tour of the exhibition for their interest in this undertaking: Columbus Museum of Art, Budd Harris Bishop, Director; Hunter Museum of Art, Cleve K. Scarbrough, Director; and Cummer Gallery of Art, Robert W. Schlageter, Director.

From the beginning this exhibition has enjoyed the enthusiastic support of key staff members of the Museum of Art, Carnegie Institute. Barbara L. Phillips, Assistant Director, who not only assumed general responsibility for coordinating the exhibition but also oversaw the production of the catalogue; Charles Cathey, Registrar; Vicky A. Clark, Curator of Education; Karen Crenshaw, Conservator; Eleanor Vuilleumier, Assistant Registrar; and Ann Scully, Exhibitions Coordinator, were all extremely helpful. Special thanks go to Jody Canoles Benedict, Secretary of the Section of Fine Arts, and to Patricia George, Secretary to the Assistant Director.

In writing and researching the catalogue the services of Gail Stavitsky, Assistant Curator of Fine Arts, were indispensable. She prepared the entries on the paintings by Hassam, Henri, and Sargent, and checked the provenances of every work. A great deal of elusive information was provided by the persons listed below without whose help this work would not have appeared: Joseph Assante, Riverdale, New York; Linda Bantel, Pennsylvania Academy of the Fine Arts, Philadelphia; Nancy Jo Barrow, Norton Gallery and School of Art, West Palm Beach, Florida; Kaycee Benton, Cragsmoor, New York; Barbara Buff, Bronxville, New York; Doreen Bolger Burke, The Metropolitan Museum of Art, New York; Kathleen Burnside, Hirschl and Adler Galleries, New York; Campanile Galleries, Chicago; Larry Casper, A.C.A. Galleries, New York; Paul Chew, Westmoreland County Museum of Art, Greensburg, Pennsylvania; Janet Fleisher, Janet Fleisher Gallery, Philadelphia; Deborah Goodwin, Cape Ann Historical Association, Gloucester, Massachusetts; Sally Gross, Allentown, Pennsylvania; Susan Harkavy, A.C.A. Galleries, New York; Lucinda Holt, The Cleveland Museum of Art; John D. Ingraham, Pierce Galleries, Hingham, Massachusetts; Frances E.

Pennington Keen, Wayne, Pennsylvania; Antoinette Kraushaar, Kraushaar Galleries, New York; Mary Guck Lane, Grand Central Art Galleries, New York; Irene Chapellier Little, Chapellier Galleries, New York; Barbara J. MacAdam, Lyme Historical Society, Old Lyme, Connecticut; John Ollman, Janet Fleisher Gallery, Philadelphia; Phoebe Peebles, Fogg Art Museum, Harvard University, Cambridge, Massachusetts; Bennard B. Perlman, Baltimore, Maryland; Patricia Jobe Pierce, Pierce Galleries, Hingham, Massachusetts; Meg Roberts, Coe Kerr Gallery, New York; Patricia Rutledge, Cincinnati Art Museum; Carol Troyen, Museum of Fine Arts, Boston; Abbot Williams Vose, Vose Galleries, Boston; and Glenn Hood, Hirschl and Adler Galleries, New York.

Most of the research for this catalogue was carried out at the Art Room of the New York Public Library (Astor, Lenox and Tilden Foundations), at the Music and Art Department of the Carnegie Library of Pittsburgh, and at the library of the Department of American Paintings and Sculpture, The Metropolitan Museum of Art, New York. We thank the various staffs of these institutions for their cheerful assistance and single out Natalie Spassky, Associate Curator, The Metropolitan Museum of Art, for her help and advice in bibliographical matters. To John Caldwell, Editor, and to Frank Garrity, Designer, go special thanks for proving such capable and good-humored colleagues.

Before a whole generation of museum curators matures it is sometimes possible to discern its leading figures. There is no doubt that Oswaldo Rodriguez has emerged as one of these rare individuals. His interests and knowledge embrace an exceptionally broad range of the fine and decorative arts, and in the American nineteenth century, his area of special expertise, his authority is very widely recognized. This exhibition and catalogue represent his last project as Curator of Fine Arts before he departs the staff of the Museum of Art, Carnegie Institute to join that of The Metropolitan Museum of Art. We wish to thank him not only for having given such thorough and intelligent attention to *Directions in American Painting 1875-1925: Works from the Collection of Dr. and Mrs. John J. McDonough*, but also to take this opportunity to express our appreciation for his many accomplishments on behalf of the Museum of Art, Carnegie Institute.

John R. Lane
Director

INTRODUCTION

Directions in American Painting 1875-1925

The paintings and watercolors in this exhibition do not represent all the trends in American painting in the years between 1875 and 1925—there are no Realist works by Winslow Homer or Thomas Eakins, no Romantic works by Albert Pinkham Ryder or Ralph Blakelock, and no Tonalist works by George Inness or Dwight Tryon—but they do admirably capture the direction taken by mainstream art during this period. This mainstream, that is to say the cluster of styles that at the time was most popular, dominated American painting between 1890 and 1915. It includes the styles of painters who were chiefly influenced by French Impressionism as well as those that sprang from its American interpretation: the style of Edmund Tarbell and his followers, now commonly referred to as the Boston School, and the style of Robert Henri and his followers, long known as the Ash Can School. Any discussion of these works must start with Impressionism and with the radical approach to the representation of light and shadow which it adopted.

Beginning in the 1860s a number of French painters, increasingly dissatisfied with the prevalent academic style and with the cultural establishment that promoted it, began to experiment with innovative painting techniques. In virtually all instances this involved a looser, more painterly handling of pigment and a concern with a realistic representation of objects not as static and detailed things but as perceived light. A number of studies dealing with color and vision provided a scientific underpinning for this movement, but it was the conscientious desire on the part of these artists to be modern and to create a style that was peculiarly of their time that provided the chief motive. Eventually, the most committed among them, having met with repeated rejection from the French artistic establishment, exhibited jointly in Paris in 1874 as a protest against the Salon. These painters had highly individual styles, but most of them, including Claude Monet, Pierre-Auguste Renoir, Camille Pissarro, and Alfred Sisley, adopted a technique of broken, juxtaposed color which, when observed at a distance, palpably reproduced the effects of light and shadow at various times of the day and in various gradations. At first their adventurous use of color, their unorthodox subject matter, and their opposition to the establishment, earned them derision and scorn, but by 1886, when they stopped showing together as a group, the Impressionists had gained the admiration and respect of most artistically knowledgeable people in France.

In America, these developments were reported in the contemporary press as amusing episodes and were not taken very seriously. In the late 1880s, however, this situation began to change as America increasingly found itself without a pictorial style that could be termed national, modern, or different. The National Academy of Design, the country's leading artistic institution, jealously guarded the realist tradition of Hudson River School painting, but by the 1880s this school, chiefly concerned with landscape painting, was played out. It had been highly suited to the contemplative approach to nature of mid-nineteenth century Romanticism, but it was not a style for a rapidly changing and developing nation.

American interest in Impressionism began in the 1870s when the Paris-based American painter Mary Cassatt became a member of the Impressionist group. As early as 1874 her work had contained the high-keyed colors favored by Edgar Degas and Monet. Cassatt, however, was very much a pioneer at a time when most American artists gravitated either to the traditional academic training available in Paris or to the dark painterly manner of the Munich School. The latter had as its chief advocate the Cincinnati artist Frank Duveneck who attracted a number of talented students to his school in Munich and who did much to wean Americans from the tight, linear style that had dominated American painting since the 1830s. Although he never embraced Impressionism himself, many of his students, among them William Merritt Chase and John H. Twachtman, became important figures in the American Impressionist movement.

For this country, the decisive turn toward Impressionism came in the 1880s. A number of events at home at the time signaled the ascendancy of the style. In 1883 a *Foreign Exhibition* in Boston contained works by Monet, Pissarro, Renoir, and Sisley, the members of the French group most committed to analytical, broken brushwork. In 1884 the exhibition held in New York to raise funds for the purchase of a pedestal for the Statue of Liberty, which had recently been donated by France, included works by Manet and Degas. In 1886 the Paris dealer Durand-Ruel organized an exhibition of about 300 Barbizon School and Impressionist paintings in New York, an event that received enormous publicity. Also during this period collectors such as Mrs. H. O. Havemeyer, Alexander Cassatt, and Erwin Davis, were making it fashionable for wealthy Americans to own French Impressionist works. The death knell of the old order in American painting, however, came when promising artists of the younger generation such as Theodore Robinson, Childe Hassam, John H. Twachtman, and Willard L. Metcalf, renounced their past training and decided to follow the tenets of Impressionism, particularly as practiced by Monet. Interestingly enough – and this is a most important factor to keep in mind in attempting to understand American Impressionism – they all did so after the French Impressionists had disbanded following their last group exhibition in 1886.

It is perhaps asking too much of artists at any given time to come to a fair assessment of the place of their particular style in the context of broader art historical currents. In the case of the American Impressionists it does not seem just to expect of them the realization that their acceptance of Impressionism had come at a time when the style was already about to enter a period of decline in its country of origin. This is especially so in view of the fact that no development looming on the American artistic horizon at the time would have prompted such a reflection. On the contrary, the crusty attitude of the leaders of the National Academy of Design, the degeneration of Hudson River School painting into easy formulas, and the vast social and economic changes in post-Civil War America, literally forced younger artists to grasp at something new and different in the way of a painting style. The general awareness in the 1870s and 80s that America lagged behind Europe in artistic education, in stylistic experimentation, and in sustaining a lively visual culture did not cause these artists to formulate a national style distinguishable from any European one but rather to attempt to catch up to what had happened there. In a sense, then, Impressionism was something American artists had to try their hand at, much as they did with Whistler's Tonalism, with the Beaux-Arts academic realism of Jean-Léon Gérôme, and with the Old Master-like styles of Edouard Manet in France and Wilhelm Leibl in Germany. The most interesting aspect of this American turn toward Impressionism, however, was its intensity. Between 1890 and 1900 Impressionism became *the* established American style, and it remained so at least until after 1920 when the modern styles introduced by the Armory Show in 1913 and the increasing popularity of the movement known as American Scene painting undermined its authority. The year 1898, when a group of Impressionists broke away from the Society of American Artists to form the Ten American Painters probably marks its artistic high point. These men formed the core group of American Impressionists and wielded enormous influence as teachers in their own private schools or in institutions such as the School of the Museum of Fine Arts in Boston and the Pennsylvania Academy of the Fine Arts. They were Childe Hassam, J. Alden Weir, John H. Twachtman, Willard L. Metcalf, Thomas Dewing, Edward Simmons, Robert Reid, Edmund Tarbell, Frank W. Benson, and Joseph R. De Camp. In 1902, after Twachtman's death, William Merritt Chase joined the group.

Once dismissed as simply a derivative style without a real place in the history of American painting, Impressionism is now recognized as a valid national expression that enjoyed enormous popularity in its own time. From the standpoint of the present it is indeed cause for wonderment that it was ever judged otherwise. The zeal with which America appropriated Impressionism was equal to or exceeded that of any other nation outside France. For many artists and critics in the period covered by this exhibition, Impressionism was not an exclusively French style but also an American one.

That America changed the accent of the language of Impressionism is a widely acknowledged fact. The American painters did not use the flickering brushwork pioneered by Monet as a device for analyzing light but rather as a device to embellish surfaces and to heighten the realistic appearance of what they represented. The emphasis on the clear perception of objects is a hallmark of their works, as is the preference for balanced and visually undisturbing compositions. In general, that aspect of French Impressionism that involved the unsentimental exploration of contemporary life in an unorthodox way was shunned by American Impressionists. If, in the context of French culture, the French Impressionists were irreverent, anti-establishment, and somewhat uncouth, in the context of American culture, the American Impressionists were tasteful, proper, and attentive to accepted notions of decorum. In their relations with each other the American Impressionists tended to be friendly, gregarious, and collegial. They frequented a number of summer colonies and often painted together outdoors. Overall, however, the chief distinguishing mark of American Impressionism was its commitment to the form of the thing seen.

This clear perception of the thing painted, observable here in the landscapes by Childe Hassam, Robert Reid, Robert Vonnoh, J. Alden Weir, and Theodore Wendel, was indeed of supreme importance to American Impressionism. Not suprisingly the two offspring of the native Impressionist style, the Boston School and the Ash Can School, further emphasized the importance of the object and transformed Impressionism by increasing rather than diminishing the painter's reliance on it. In content and sensibility these schools could not have been more opposed: the Boston painters (Joseph Rodefer De Camp, William M. Paxton) emphasized gentility, exoticism, subdued light, prettiness, and careful execution, while the Ash Can artists (George Bellows, Robert Henri) preferred bluntness, sharply contrasted colors, quick and broad execution, and frequently unattractive urban subject matter. Yet, in a very basic way, both of them made Impressionism look back to older realist traditions: in the case of the Boston School to Vermeer and other Dutch 17th-century painters of interiors and in the case of the Ash Can School to Velázquez and Manet. This course of events permits us to formulate the difference between American and French Impressionism in a more general and conceptual way: whereas the French style contained within itself many of the elements of Postimpressionism, Fauvism, Futurism, and even abstraction, for all of which it acted as a precursor and a catalyst, the American interpretation of it lacked these forward-looking elements and instead pointed towards a re-affirmation of realism and pictorial content. Neither the artists nor the country as a whole was ready for modernism or for the underlying attitudes that fueled it. Intellectual restlessness, innovation as a desired end in itself, secularism, and the relentless questioning of long held principles—not only in art but also in politics, religion, and personal conduct—were not for the American Impressionists, most of whom led outer and inner lives of remarkable regularity and stability. The progress of Impressionism in the United States was therefore not marked by revolutionary episodes. Once the style gained general acceptance in the 1890s it followed a notably placid line of development not unlike the sensibility behind the paintings themselves. The perceptive critic Christian Brinton, after viewing the predominantly Impressionist American paintings exhibited at the San Francisco International Exposition in 1915, sensed this and noted that while he could not "describe the paintings at the Panama-Pacific Exposition as being in any degree radical or modernistic, still they were sufficiently indicative of the fact that art in America is progressing along normal, wholesome lines" (*Impressions of the Art at the Panama-Pacific Exposition* [1916], p. 98).

For many, this normal, wholesome quality of American Impressionism long stood as a barrier to its appreciation. By and large, from the 1930s until very recently, published histories of American art ignored the movement or gave it scant attention. Thomas Eakins, Winslow Homer, and Albert Pinkham Ryder, the figures that were made to bridge the gap between the late Hudson River School and the early modernists who grouped themselves around the photographer and dealer Alfred Stieglitz, were seen as giants standing in splendid isolation. The expatriate painters, J. A. M. Whistler, John Singer Sargent, and Mary Cassatt, were never ignored because their achievements were of international significance, but their success abroad was never deemed too relevant to developments at home. Thus, by implication, Impressionism in America was treated as an artistic aberration that had been false to the American spirit. Its historical profile, which in terms of the number of works produced and of their chronological span was a considerable one, was made to appear insignificant. This treatment of events was a deplorable one; it not only diminished the actual importance of American Impressionism but also that of the predominantly academic American painting that had preceded it in the 1870s and 80s. It made any accurate understanding of the careers of Eakins, Homer, and Ryder impossible and, more importantly, it consigned to obscurity a large number of art works of great beauty.

In a sense the state of neglect in which American Impressionism found itself between about 1930 and 1970 was not different from that in which the Hudson River School languished between 1880 and 1960. In both cases the native paintings were perceived as echoes of foreign styles that failed to capture the complex resonance of European ones. It did not seem to make a difference that some works executed by the American followers of the European leaders were in fact superior to some works produced by those leaders or that, at times, their interpretations of European styles yielded something recognizably different. The chief criterion for judging quality was not an independent assessment of individual works of art but whether the artist in question had pioneered a major stylistic innovation. To a great extent the blame for this general outlook may be placed squarely on the shoulders of art historians. Proceeding along biographical lines and always faced with large quantities of works of variable quality, they reduced the progress of Western painting from Jacques-Louis David to Jackson Pollock to a series of changes of style, each associated with the names of a few great artists. This approach stressed continuity and the inexorable march of art toward the painting of our own day. Unfortunately for this view of things the past was forsaken by the present. Abstraction, and modernism itself, reached a crisis point in the 1970s as artists began to experiment with the eclecticism of realist styles that had been relegated to the dustbin of art history. In this general mood of reappraisal, the virtues of good painting, regardless of the artist involved and of whether the style was progressive or not, have increasingly come to be recognized. In American art in particular the condemnation of its largely derivative nature has given way to an exploration of the native inflections in, or native interpretations of, the various borrowed styles. Since the mid 60s Hudson River School painting has benefited enormously from this change in the cultural climate. Now a similar process is underway with respect to American Impressionism. Its peculiarly American qualities—the decorative surfaces, the pervasive mood of well-being, the straightforwardness of the compositions, the harmony of the color schemes, and the emphasis on the easy perception of objects—are beginning to be seen as a significant national expression. The tendency today is toward serious acceptance of the style as a fit subject for investigation, study, and enjoyment. The result has been a nearly total rehabilitation of the painters who belonged to the Ten and increased attention paid to late practitioners of Impressionism such as Frederick Frieseke, Richard E. Miller, Edward Redfield, and Edward Potthast. The Ash Can School painters, because their subject matter was always regarded as quintessentially American and worthy of attention, were never ignored as the Ten and their followers were. Consequently, the continued appreciation of their paintings does not constitute a radical reevaluation. The Boston School painters, on the other hand, have literally been restored to the rank of real artists and have regained the historical presence which they very nearly lost. They were, in a sense, the distillers of the sensibility that had informed American Impressionism all along. As the Ash Can School painters turned to the slums and tenements of New York City in search of the biting edge they felt was missing in American art (and in doing so took a significant step toward modernity), the Boston School painters retreated to the marvelously feminine world of upper class boudoirs and drawing rooms. They kept this tradition alive in spite of the multitude of changes that occurred in American art in the 1930s and 40s and nurtured a progeny that is still adhering to the general principles of the style.

CATALOGUE

George Bellows
(1882-1925)

Lillian was painted at Camden, Maine, in the summer of 1916. Although the identity of the sitter is not known, it is possible that she was either a local resident or one of Bellows' models. Her portrait was not a commissioned work, and remained in the possession of the artist and his family until the 1950s.

Although Bellows painted portraits throughout his career, it was not until about 1913 that he developed a keen interest in the genre. From this time on, his portraits became more complex both coloristically and formally, and they began to show a monumentality of conception that reflected the artist's interest in the portraits of Hals, Velázquez, and Titian. As in the portrait of Geraldine Lee (1914, Butler Institute of American Art, Youngstown, Ohio), Bellows has here placed the sitter against an undefined background that does not place the figure in relief but rather fills out the work as an arrangement of flat shapes and colors. The execution is quick and fluid, and at times the surface of the panel is left unpainted to emphasize further the abstract quality of the work. Of interest also are the still-life passages in the hat held by Lillian and in the vase of flowers on the table next to her. This interest in portrait accessories would grow in the following years and would lead to their abundant use in portraits such as *Mrs. T. in Cream Silk* (1919, Hirshhorn Museum and Sculpture Garden, Washington, D.C.) and *Lady Jean* (1924, Yale University Art Gallery, New Haven, Connecticut).

References:
George Bellows, *Book B* (Private list of paintings kept by the artist), ms. in possession of H.V. Allison and Co., New York, p. 53, lists it and establishes when and where painted; "Eleventh Annual Exhibition of Selected Paintings by American Artists at the Albright Art Gallery", *Academy Notes* 12 (July-September 1917), p. 94, says "In 'Lillian' George Bellows has gone below the surface and, painting with his usual virtuosity, shows a great feeling for his subject"; Emma S. Bellows, *The Paintings of George Bellows* (1929), no. 57.

Exhibited:
Corcoran Gallery of Art, Washington, D.C., 1916-1917, *6th Annual Exhibition of Oil Paintings by Contemporary American Artists*, no. 6; Albright Art Gallery, Buffalo Fine Arts Academy, Buffalo, New York, 1917, *11th Annual Exhibition of Selected Paintings by American Artists*, no. 12, ill. p. 49, Milch Galleries, New York, 1918, *George Bellows*, no. 8, ill. on cover; Albright Art Gallery, Buffalo Fine Arts Academy, Buffalo, New York, 1919, *Exhibition of Paintings by George Bellows*, No. 16; H.V. Allison and Co., Inc., New York, 1958, *George Bellows*, no. 6; The Westmoreland County Museum of Art, Greensburg, Pennsylvania, 1977, *The Collection of the Virgnia Steel Scott Foundation, Pasadena, California*, no. 3.

Ex coll.:
Estate of the artist; H. V. Allison and Co., Inc., New York, 1958; Mrs. Victoria Dreyfus, Brewster, New York; sale, Sotheby Parke-Bernet, Inc., New York, October 28, 1976, no. 152; The Virginia Steel Scott Foundation, Pasadena, California, 1976-79; sale, Christie's, New York, May 23, 1979, no. 262; Dr. and Mrs. John J. McDonough, Youngstown, Ohio.

Lillian
1916

oil on panel
38 x 30 in. (96.5 x 76.2 cm.)
Signed, lower left: Geo. Bellows
Signed and inscribed on back: Lillian/Geo. Bellows/146 E. 19 St./N.Y.

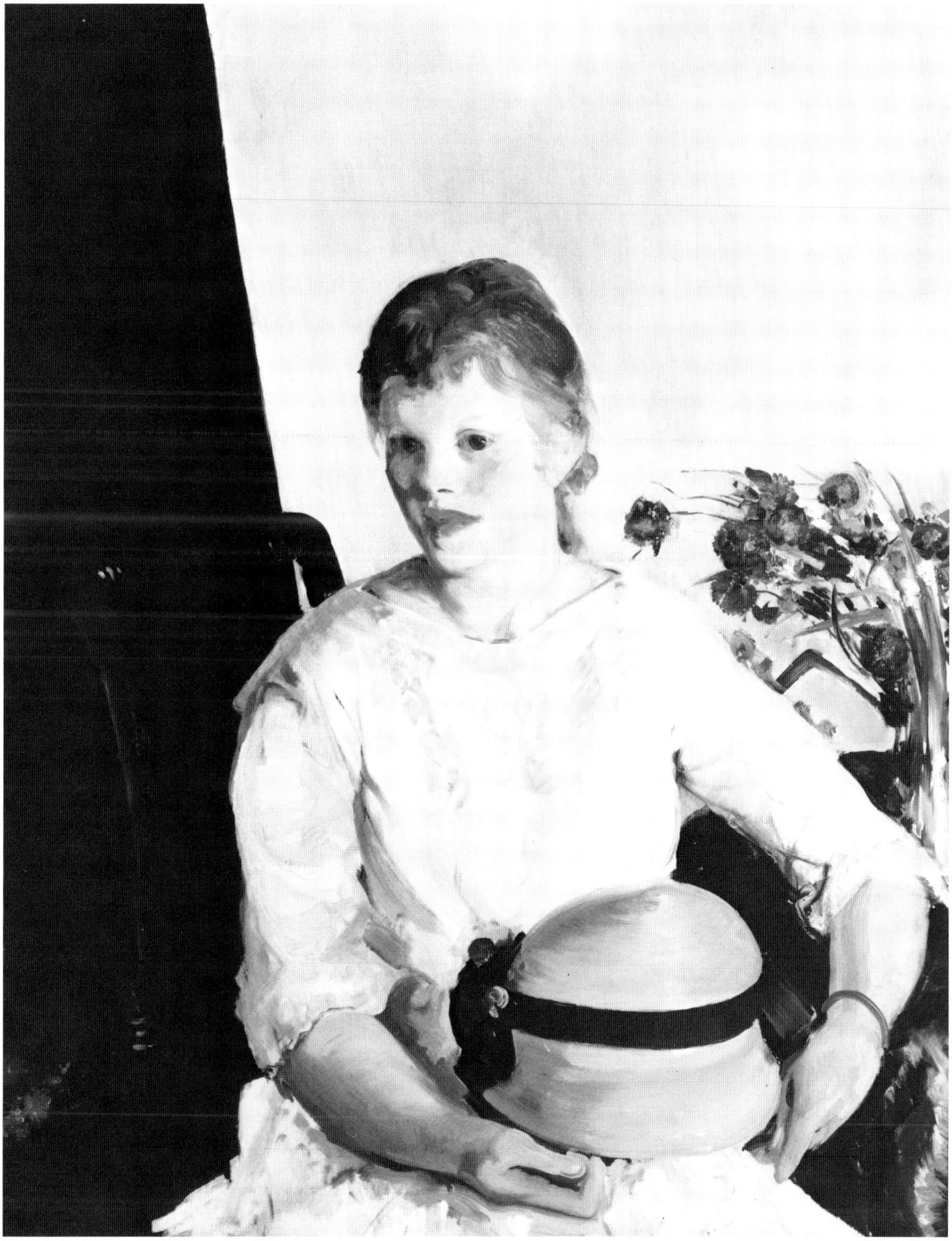

Dennis Miller Bunker
(1861-1890)

Sometime between his return to America in 1885 and his visit to John Singer Sargent in the summer of 1888, Bunker painted a number of pictures depicting abandoned, beached boats. As William H. Gerdts has noted, these works "have a haunting, desolate quality which deserves greater study," but they are more related to Barbizon School painting than to Impressionism (William H. Gerdts, *American Impressionism* [1980], p. 41). It was only after his summer with Sargent at Calcot in England that Bunker began to paint in an impressionist manner that was clearly derived from Sargent's.

Although they are related to an American tradition of beached boat paintings that includes works by Fitz Hugh Lane, Martin Johnson Heade, and Winslow Homer, Bunker's pictures communicate a special feeling of poignancy. Perhaps they are emblematic of his own condition at this time. As Bunker's biographer wrote: "It would be impossible to arrive at any understanding of Bunker's attitude toward life without a full realization of the extent to which he was tortured by ill health. His own outward appearance did not suggest this to his friends. The melancholy, often verging on despair, to which he was so frequently subject, was unquestionably intensified by his physical condition. And the constantly recurring headaches and bouts of indigestion interfered with his enjoyment of the opportunities that were open to him" (R.H. Ives Gammell, *Dennis Miller Bunker* [1953], p. 25). It does not seem surprising, therefore, that someone in such a distressed physical state should have found the image of a decaying, abandoned boat especially meaningful.

References:
Steven Straw Company, Inc., Newburyport Massachusetts, *American Selections* (1978), unpaged, ill. in color.

Exhibited:
St. Botolph Club, Boston, 1891, *Exhibition of the Pictures of Dennis Miller Bunker*, no. 56, as *A Hulk*, possibly this work; New Britain Museum of American Art, New Britain, Connecticut, and Davis and Long Company, Inc., New York, 1978, *Dennis Miller Bunker Rediscovered*, no. 22.

Ex coll.:
James McGrath, Boston; Vose Galleries, Inc., Boston, about 1970; Jeffrey R. Brown, Long Meadow, Massachusetts, about 1973; Steven Straw Company, Inc., Newburyport, Massachusetts; sale, Butterfield and Butterfield, Inc., San Francisco, October 8, 1980, no. 165; Dr. and Mrs. John J. McDonough, Youngstown, Ohio.

Old Hulks
c. 1887

oil on canvas
14 x 20½ in. (35.6 x 52.1 cm.)
Signed, lower right: DB

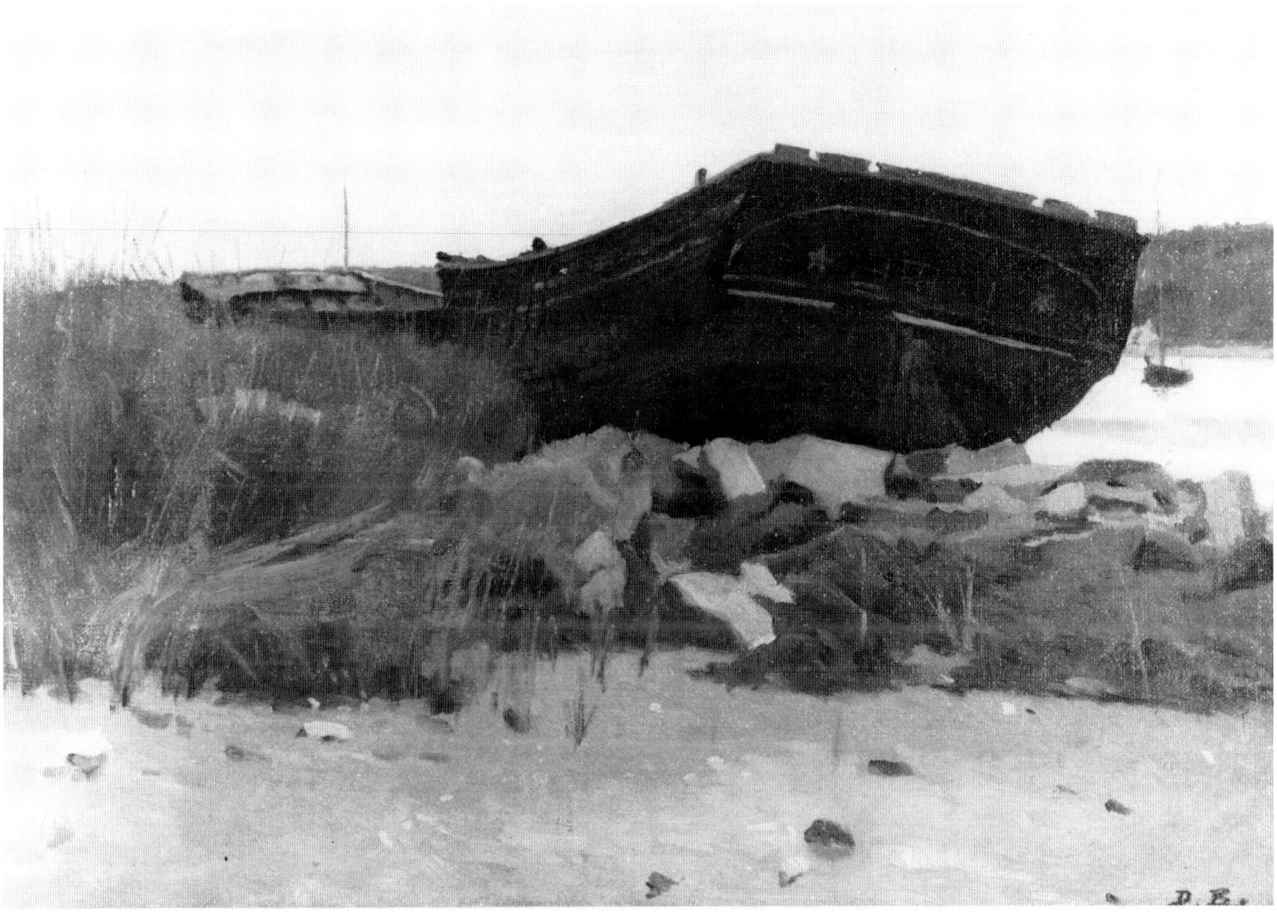

Theodore Earl Butler
(1860-1936)

This work probably depicts Butler's second wife, Marthe Hoschedé-Monet, whom he married in 1901. She was the sister of Butler's first wife Suzanne and the stepdaughter of Claude Monet. During her sister's long illness, which terminated in Suzanne's death in 1899, Marthe Hoschedé-Monet took care of her sister's children, James and Lili, and generally managed the Butler house in Giverny. She was, with James and Lili, frequently painted by Butler in works such as *Girl in Lavender, Seated at Desk*, which depict scenes in Butler's house.

Despite his close family relations with Monet, Butler seldom discussed painting with the grand old man of Impressionism. They painted separately, exhibited separately, and do not appear to have shown each other their work. Thus, Butler's works of 1901-13, generally accepted as the best of his painting career, are not so much indebted to the later style of Monet as to the paintings of Edouard Vuillard and other members of the *Nabis*. Butler's sense of color, however, was entirely his own, as this work, with its predominant lavender tones interspersed throughout a tapestry of greens, oranges, and yellows, amply bears out. Although in Butler's paintings the outline of forms is fairly clear, realistic modeling within those outlines takes second place to his lively and adventurous arrangements of color.

References:
Sally Gross, personal communication with the author, February 1, 1982, says the subject is probably Butler's wife Marthe rather than his daughter Lili who is usually depicted by Butler in a school dress.

Exhibited:
Slatkin Galleries, New York, 1960, *Claude Monet and the Giverny Artists*, no. 20; Janet Fleisher Gallery, Philadelphia, 1965, *Theodore Earl Butler*, no. 11.

Ex coll.:
Michel Monet, Giverny; Janet Fleisher Gallery, Philadelphia, until 1967; Dr. Albert Kaplan, Philadelphia; sale, Samuel T. Freeman and Company, Inc., Philadelphia, April 20, 21, 1978, no. 412 as *Girl in Lavender, Seated at Desk*; Dr. and Mrs. John J. McDonough, Youngstown, Ohio.

Girl in Lavender, Seated at Desk
1908

oil on canvas
29 x 23¼ in. (73.7 x 59.1 cm.)
Signed, lower left: T. E. Butler '08

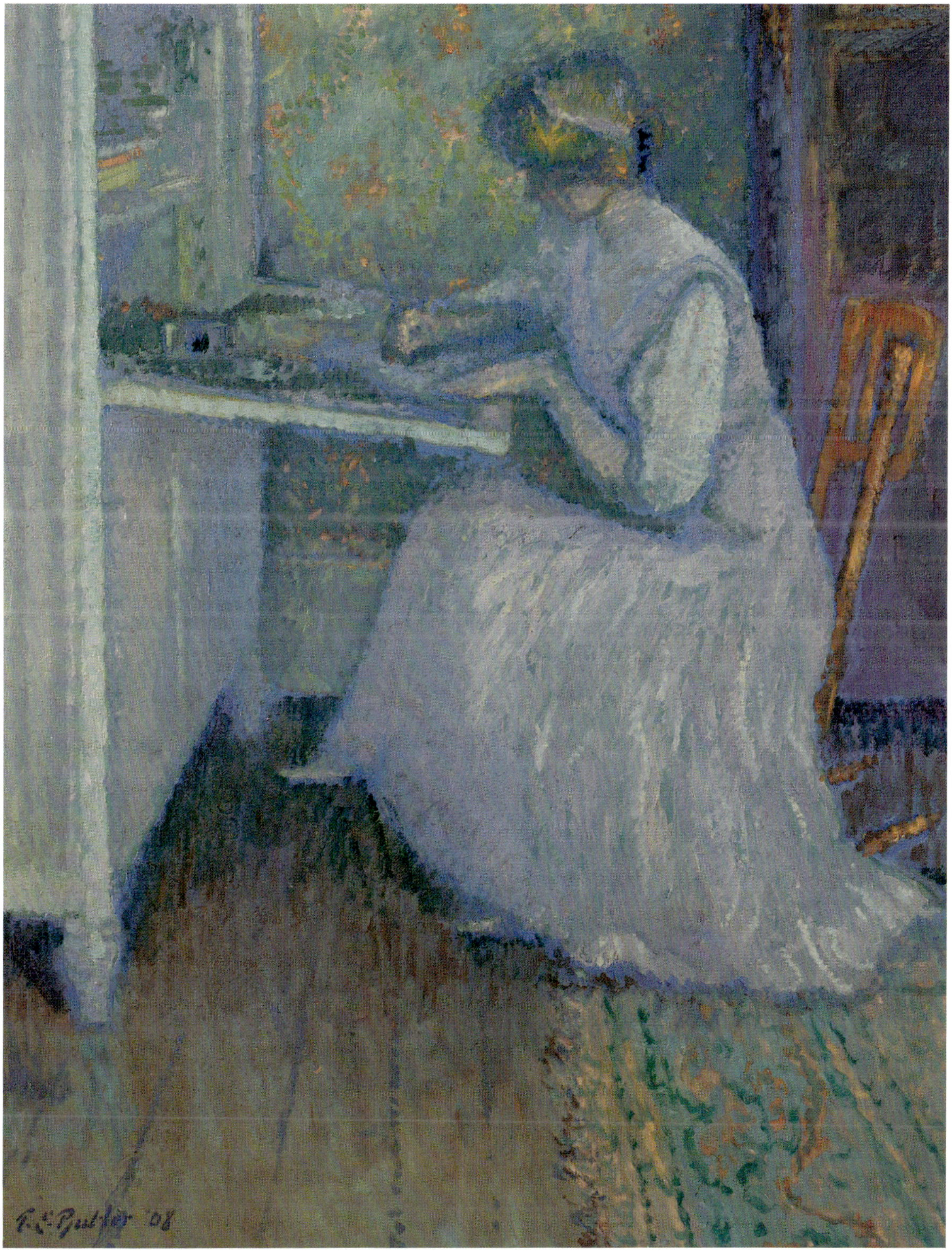

Mary Stevenson Cassatt (1844-1926)

Although in her later years Mary Cassatt devoted herself to painting pictures of mothers and children, from time to time she executed a work containing a single, usually female, figure. Here, as is usual in her works, the theme of a woman arranging her hair while looking in a mirror is an intensely feminine one. This subject, popularized by the paintings and pastels of Degas depicting ladies in their boudoirs before or after a bath, became a prevalent one around the turn of the century and was exploited by American painters, such as Richard Miller and Frederick Frieseke, as well as French ones, such as Pierre Bonnard. Why Cassatt turned to this theme at this point in her career is not known, but it is clear that her choice—with its definite reference to the traditional iconography of vanity—was deliberate. Cassatt does not appear to have used mothers with their own children in the paintings for which she is best known but unrelated models of local peasant origin. In the case of *Antoinette at Her Dressing Table* it is certain that the girl did not own any of the clothes or accessories seen in the work, and that the picture is not meant to be a portrait. Rather, Antoinette is engaged in a bit of harmless pretending arranged by Cassatt. Perhaps it is her innocent complicity that accounts for the sense of playfulness communicated by the picture.

The Empire-style dressing table seen here was also prominently employed by Cassatt in *The Oval Mirror* (1901, Metropolitan Museum of Art, New York). That work had been highly praised by Degas who discussed every aspect of it with her and made no secret of his approval (Breeskin, 1970, p. 17). It is thus likely that an important motive behind the making of this painting was Cassatt's desire to attempt a variation of the figures-with-dressing-table theme which had so impressed her mentor. In this work, however, the brushwork is bolder and the colors used are much stronger.

References:
Achille Ségard, *Un peintre des Enfants et des Mères—Mary Cassatt* (1913), ill. opposite p. 168; Clara MacChesney, "Mary Cassatt & Her Work," *Arts and Decoration* 3 (June 1913), p. 265; André Mellerio, "Mary Cassatt," *L'Art et les Artistes* 12 (November 1919), pp. 69-75; Edith Valerio, *Mary Cassatt* (1930), pl. 30; Adelyn D. Breeskin, *Mary Cassatt* (1970), p. 17, no. 543.

Exhibited:
Cleveland Museum of Art, 1916, *Inaugural Exhibition*, p. 123, no. 23, as *Femme à sa Toilette*; Corcoran Gallery of Art, Washington, D.C., 1916-1917, *6th Annual Exhibition of Oil Paintings by Contemporary American Artists*, no. 364; Pennsylvania Academy of the Fine Arts, Philadelphia, 1917, *112th Annual Exhibition*, no. 99; Baltimore Museum of Art, 1968, *From El Greco to Pollock*, no. 50; Joslyn Art Museum, Omaha, Nebraska, 1969, *Mary Cassatt among the Impressionists*, no. 1; National Gallery of Art, Washinton, D.C., 1970, *Mary Cassatt*, no. 75; Museum of Fine Arts, Boston, 1978, *Mary Cassatt at Home*, no. 31; Isetan Museum of Art, Tokyo and Nara Prefectural Museum of Art, 1981, *The Art of Mary Cassatt*, p. 109, ill. in color, pl. 46; C. W. Post Art Gallery, Long Island University, Greenvale, New York, 1981, *Madame in Her Boudoir*, unpaged, ill. in color.

Ex coll.:
The artist; Durand-Ruel, Paris, 1910; Durand-Ruel, Inc., New York; Mrs. Nelson Robinson, New York, 1910; Durand-Ruel, Inc., New York, 1912; private collection, Switzerland, 1948; Dr. Samuel E. Johnson, Chicago; Steven Straw Company, Inc., Newburyport, Massachusetts, 1978; Dr. and Mrs. John J. McDonough, Youngstown, Ohio.

Antoinette at Her Dressing Table
c. 1909

oil on canvas
$36\frac{1}{2}$ x $28\frac{1}{2}$ in. (92.7 x 72.4 cm.)
Signed, lower right: Mary Cassatt

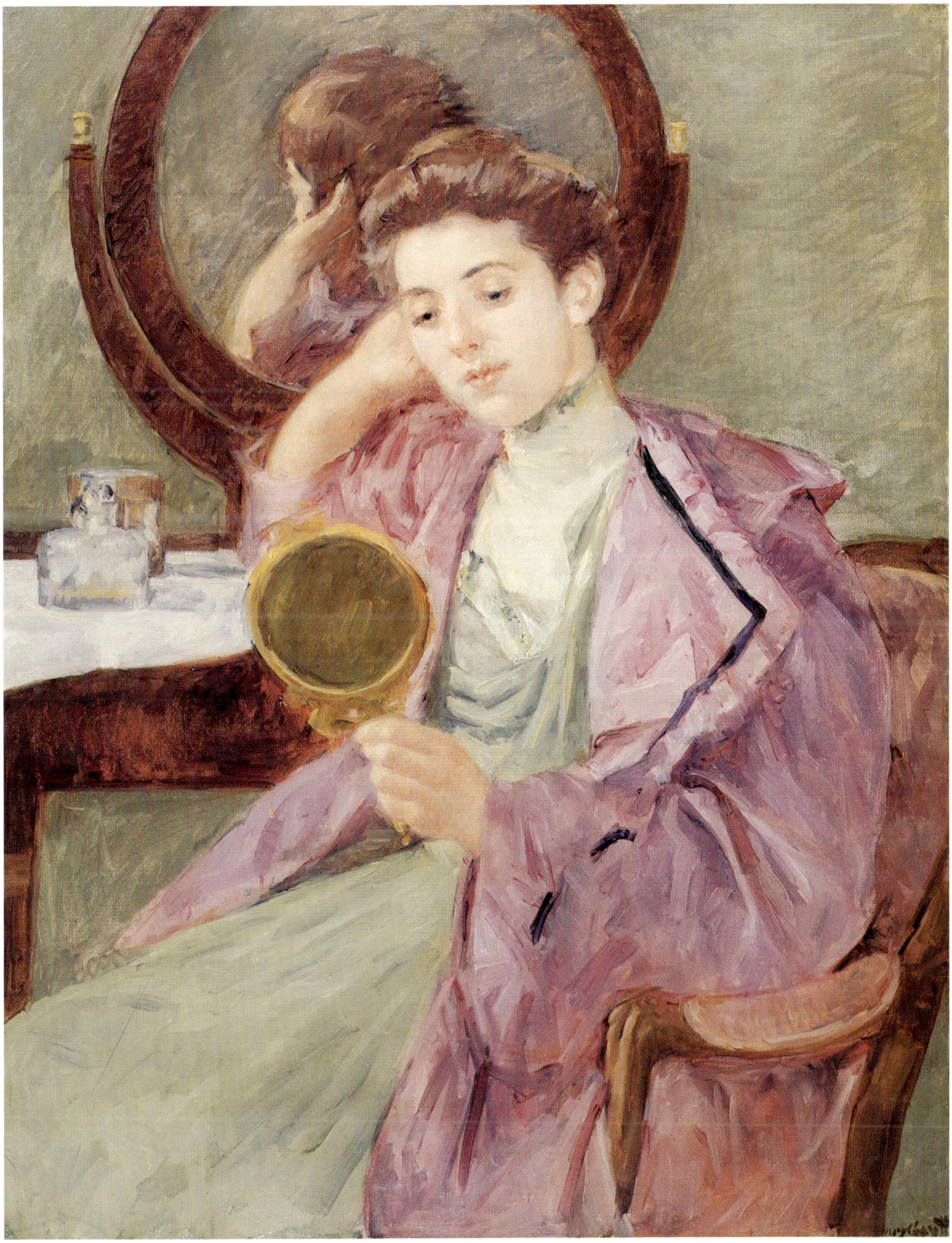

William Merritt Chase
(1849-1916)

Frances Vonlohr Earle was the daughter of the Philadelphia financier and banker George Earle. According to family tradition she was her father's favorite daughter and a woman of high spirits. Her hobby was driving carriages, and she frequently exhibited her carriage horses at the Devon, Pennsylvania, horse show. She was among the first Philadelphia women to own an automobile and during World War I was a volunteer driver for the Red Cross. About 1908 she married Lawrence Dilworth Beggs of Pittsburgh; they had two children. She died in 1919 at her home in Philadelphia of influenza and in childbirth. Her brother George H. Earle was a governor of Pennsylvania.

Painted when the sitter was seventeen, this portrait is an outstanding example of the artist's mature style. The critic William Howe Downes, writing in 1909 of Chase's recent works, including this portrait, summarized that style as follows: "[It] is one in which brilliancy, gayety [sic] and charm are often the dominant notes, in which lightness of touch, clearness of expression and a happy freedom of treatment are combined with great taste and elegance. An accomplished painter, he avoids, by instinct, complicated questions, metaphysics, dealing rather with the phenomena which are pictorially effective by virtue of their form, color, light and shade, and giving us a faithful and enthusiastic rendering of the external world" (Downes, 1909, p. xxix). In this portrait, Chase's free brushwork is particularly evident in the lace ruffles of Miss Earle's debutante dress and in the feather in her hat. The influence of Velázquez in this respect, as well as in the positioning of the figure against a dark background, is also clear. Originally, Chase had intended the billowing red cloak to fill the lower left corner of the painting, but he later changed his mind and painted this section over in the black-brown tones of the background.

References:
William Howe Downes, "William Merritt Chase, a Typical American Artist," *International Studio* 39 (December 1909), p. xxxii, ill. p. xxxv, says: "Miss Earle, of Philadelphia is a three-quarters-length standing figure of a slender, graceful, elegant young lady in a white gown and big hat with a white feather, the dark cloak being thrown back and lightly held by one hand. It is a work of distinct charm and of a lively personality"; Ronald G. Pisano, letter to Robert D. Schwartz, October 20, 1980, copy in Dr. John J. McDonough files, says this portrait is no. 912/895 in the catalogue raisonné of Chase's work he is compiling; Victoria Donohoe, *Philadelphia Inquirer*, December 5, 1980, in a review of the exhibition at Frank S. Schwartz & Son, Inc., notes that it is "the centerpiece of the golden anniversary show of varied American paintings and watercolors at Schwartz"; Mrs. Frances E. Pennington Keen, personal communication with author, February 17, 1982, gives biographical details about the subject.

Exhibited:
Pennsylvania Academy of the Fine Arts, Philadelphia, 1906, *101st Annual Exhibition*, no. 516, lent by George H. Earle, Jr., Esq.; Frank S. Schwartz & Son, Inc., Philadelphia, 1980, *In Celebration of Fifty Years, 1930-1980*, no. 1.

Ex coll.:
George H. Earle, Jr., Philadelphia; his granddaughter, the sitter's daughter, Mrs. Louise Dilworth Beggs Goodall, Philadelphia; her daughter, Mrs. Frances E. Pennington Keen, Wayne, Pennsylvania; Frank S. Schwartz & Son, Inc., Philadelphia, until 1981; Dr. and Mrs. John J. McDonough, Youngstown, Ohio.

Frances V. Earle
1905

oil on canvas
60 x 36 in. (152.4 x 91.4 cm.)
Signed and dated, lower left: W^{m} M Chase.
Signed, dated, and inscribed, on back: Francis Von Lohr Earle/
Daughter of George H. Earl jr./Age 17./Painted by W.M. Chase/1905.

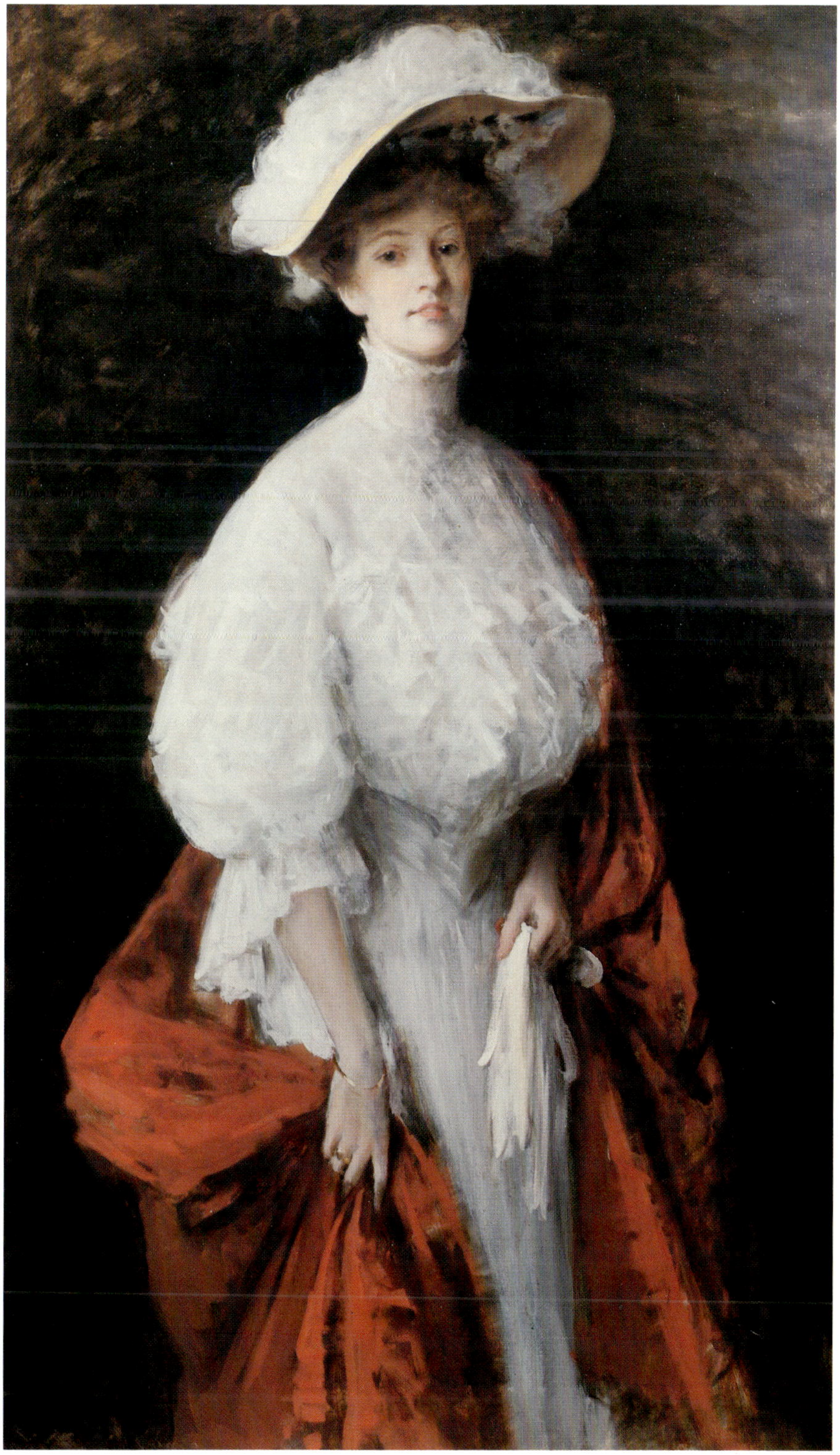

Paul Cornoyer
(1864-1923)

Cornoyer was not a leading artistic figure during his lifetime but rather a respected professional whose city views of New York sold steadily and well. As did many of his contemporaries he practiced a modified Impressionism that concerned itself with the representation of light – especially sunlight – and used the Impressionists' palette, but he did not adopt the disengaged brushwork and the analytical juxtaposition of color of Monet's mature style. The highpoint of his career was probably the one-man exhibition he was given at the Albright Art Gallery in Buffalo in 1908. A published commentary on that exhibition, describing a work that is certainly this one, provides the only information about its original title and approximate date of execution: "A third canvas presents 'A Late Afternoon in Washington Square.' The last rays of the setting sun gild the top of the Washington Arch and the upper portion of the University buildings on the east side of the Square. They also give glowing color to the branches of the budding trees in the middle-ground. The lower portion of the canvas is in a half-light, and here, on the broad walks along the foreground, figures, moving about, give touches of color – repeating to some extent the brightness of the upper portion of the canvas" (*Academy Notes*, 1908, pp. 98-99).

The same unidentified author aptly summarized Cornoyer's achievement as follows: "Mr. Cornoyer has devoted himself largely to the representation of street scenes and effects, and in this direction he is not surpassed by any other American painter. He possesses that rare faculty of knowing what to leave out in matters of detail – and he well understands the value and the legitimate scope of suggestion. His representations are not at all literal in their details, yet they convey the impression of literalness when seen from the proper distance. They not only are truthful portrayals, but they show us scenes as the artist saw them, and, especially, as they appealed to his poetic feeling and to his sensitive appreciation of beautiful color" (*Academy Notes*, 1908, p. 97).

References:
"Two Special Exhibitions," *Academy Notes* 4 (December 1908), pp. 97-100.

Exhibited:
Albright Art Gallery, Buffalo Fine Arts Academy, Buffalo, New York, 1908, *A Collection of Oil Paintings by Paul Cornoyer*, no. 16, as *Late Afternoon – Washington Square*.

Ex coll.:
Edward L. Barlow, North Carolina, until 1979; sale, Sotheby Parke-Bernet, Inc. (PB 84), January 23, 1979, no. 124; Dr. and Mrs. John J. McDonough, Youngstown, Ohio.

Late Afternoon, Washington Square
c. 1908

oil on canvas
22 x 26 in. (55.9 x 66 cm.)
Signed, lower left: Paul Cornoyer

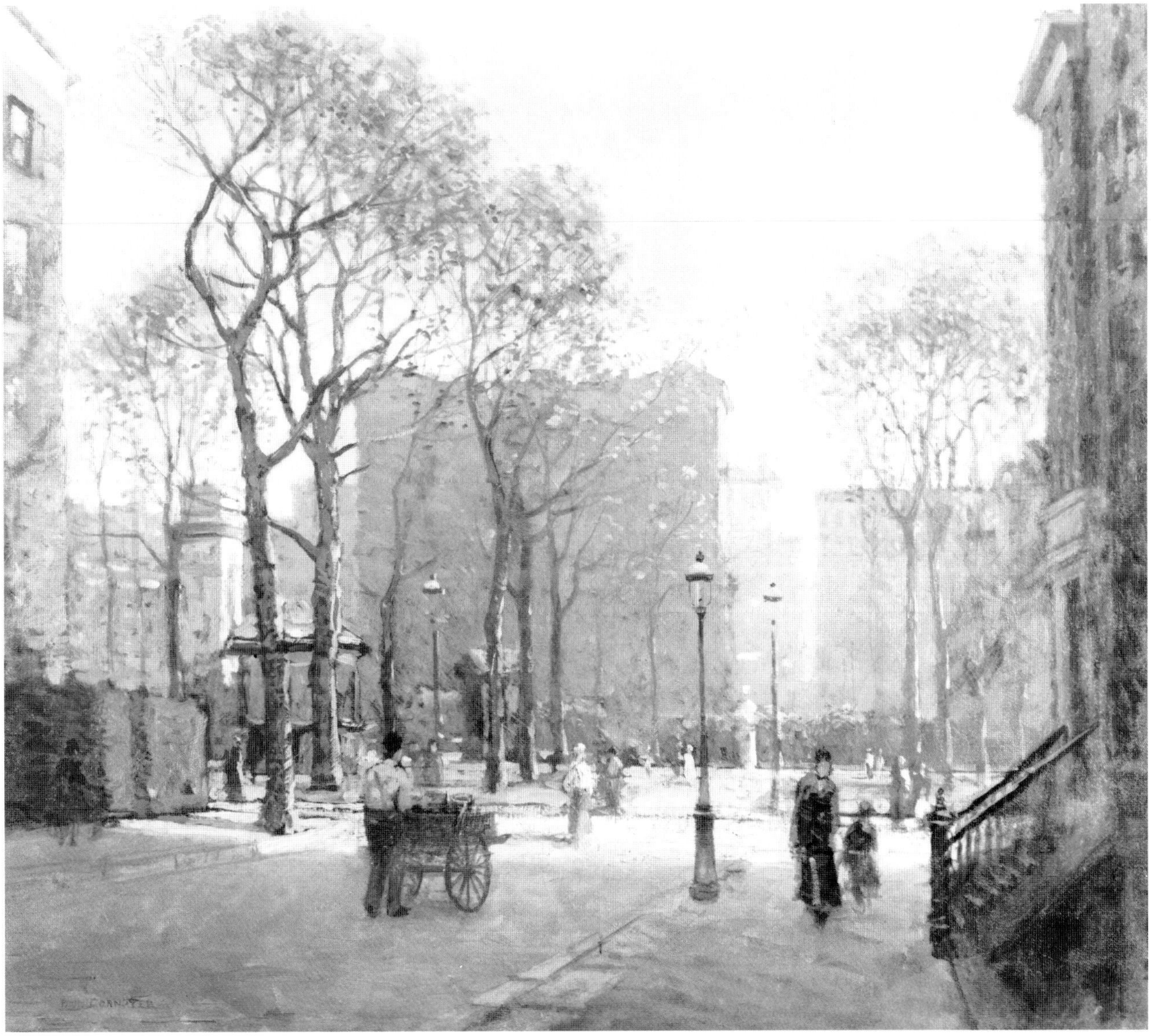

Charles Courtney Curran
(1861-1942)

The paintings for which Charles Courtney Curran is now best known, representations of healthy young women in the sun-filled, crisp atmosphere of mountaintops, were painted by him from about 1905 on at the artists' colony of Cragsmoor, New York. Located in Ulster County on a plateau in the Shawangunk Mountains, Cragsmoor was frequented in the summertime by a number of artists including Curran, Edward Lamson Henry, Eliza Greatorex, J.G. Brown, and Arthur I. Keller. They were attracted by the unobstructed views of the surrounding valleys and mountains, the frequently changing light, and the constantly blowing cool breezes. By and large, they were established artists working in academic styles and associated with the National Academy of Design (Barbara Buff, "Cragsmoor, An Early American Art Colony," *Antiques* 114 [November 1978], pp. 1056-1067).

Painted on the grounds of the Cragsmoor Inn and showing a panoramic view of the Shawangunk Mountains in the distance, this work is typical of the finest works painted by Curran in this locale. As do many of these paintings, it depicts his daughter Emily. Its vivid greens, its dramatically positioned figures, and its clear and palpable atmosphere recall Theodore Dreiser's perceptive comment made about Curran's works of the 1890s: "[His pictures] seek out a lightness and brightness in life, noted of all men, yet seldom compounded effectively in a painting" (Theodore Dreiser, "C.C. Curran," *Truth* 18 [September 1899], p. 228).

References:
Kaycee Benton, letter to author, February 4, 1982 identifies the figure and location, gives provenance and exhibition history and notes that Curran's Record Book (ms. in her possession) states that the work was also exhibited at the New York Public Library and at the Dayton Art Institute with no dates given.

Exhibited:
Salmagundi Club, New York, 1922, *Summer Exhibition*, no cat.; Cragsmoor Free Library, Cragsmoor, New York, 1975, *Cragsmoor Artists Past and Present, 1885-1975*, no cat.; Cragsmoor Free Library, Cragsmoor, New York, 1976, *An Exhibition of Cragsmoor Artists, 1870s through 1930s*, no cat.

Ex coll.:
Estate of the artist; his daughter Emily Curran, until 1972; Kaycee Benton, Cragsmoor, New York; Pierce Galleries, Inc., Hingham, Massachusetts, until 1979; sale, Barridoff Galleries, Inc., Portland, Maine, April 17, 1979, no. 43; Dr. and Mrs. John J. McDonough, Youngstown, Ohio.

May Afternoon
1916

oil on canvas
20 x 30 in. (50.8 x 76.2 cm.)
Signed and dated, lower left: Charles C. Curran/1916

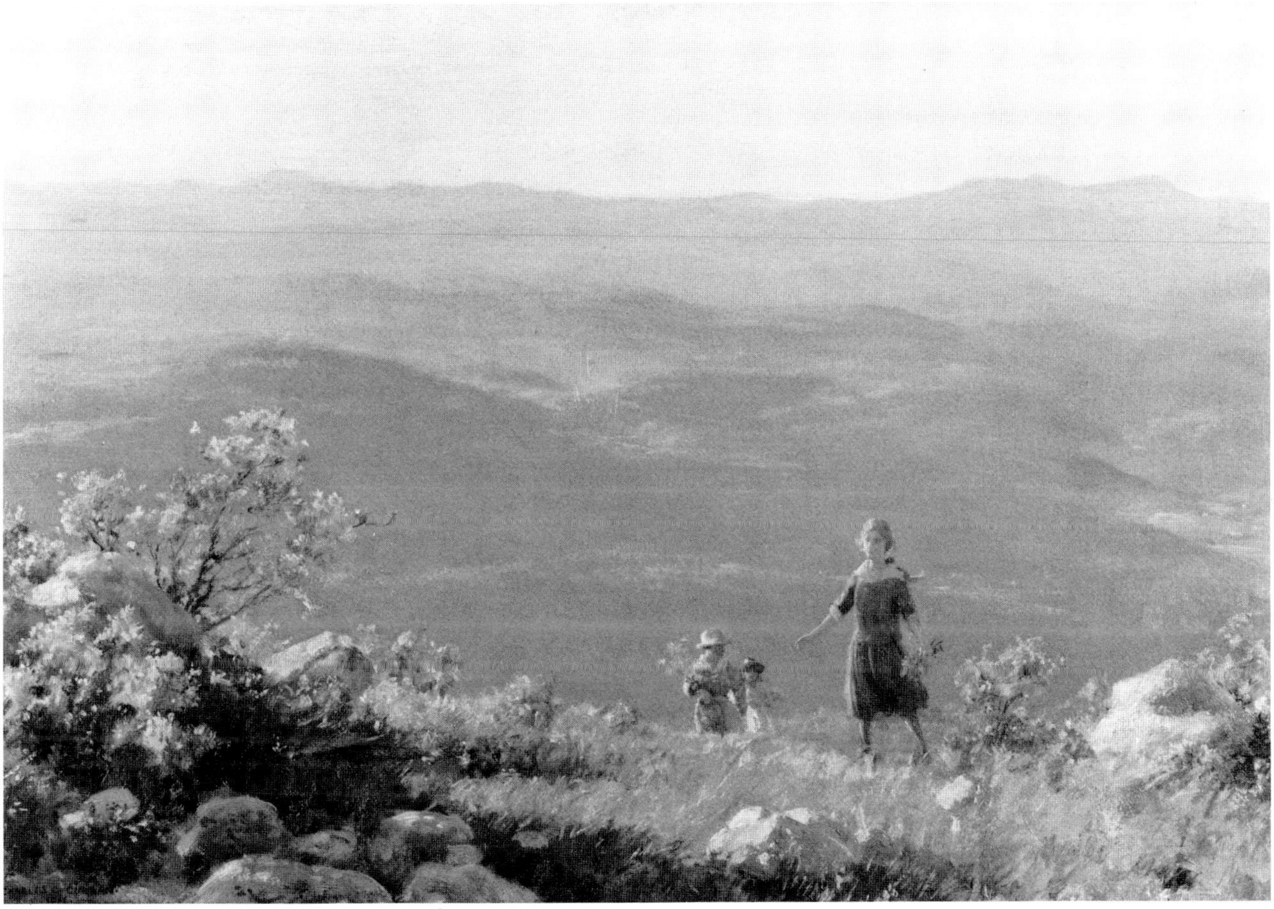

Joseph Rodefer De Camp (1858-1923)

One of the founding members of the Ten American Painters, De Camp belonged to the section of the group that shunned the broken brushwork of Impressionism and instead adhered to more traditional principles of draftsmanship and execution. These artists were Edmund C. Tarbell, Frank W. Benson, Thomas W. Dewing, and De Camp. With the exception of Dewing, they were the leading members of what is now known as the Boston School. They specialized in beautifully and softly finished interior scenes featuring women at leisure, often in a contemplative attitude, and in subdued still-lifes with exotic objects. They were all influenced by the paintings of Vermeer and the Dutch Little Masters. One of the early members of the Boston School, De Camp counted among his students William M. Paxton, but his influence on others was not great. He made a living for the most part as a portrait-painter, and his subject paintings—a large number of which were burned in a studio fire in 1904—are now fairly rare.

La Penserosa (the thoughtful one) was probably painted between 1904, the year of the studio fire, and 1908, the year it was exhibited at the Pennsylvania Academy of the Fine Arts. It is a distillation of De Camp's style: the subject is a woman, she is in a thoughtful mood, she is painted in an exceedingly careful manner, and she stands in an interior with the sunlight streaming in from one direction. How De Camp went about achieving these results was elucidated by Rose Berry in 1923: "De Camp seldom required a fixed, rigid pose of his model. He walked around the sitter, he felt of the head, discovered the texture of the ear, examined its placement upon the head, and proceeded in general with much the line of attack which a sculptor takes. He was painstaking, but so much the virtuoso that in his task accomplished there was no evidence of hesitancy, but every appearance of its having been achieved with the greatest ease" (Rose V.S. Berry, "Joseph De Camp: Painter and Man," *American Magazine of Art* 14 [April 1923], pp. 183-184).

References:
William Howe Downes, "Joseph De Camp and His Work," *Art and Progress* 4 (April 1913), p. 921, says *La Penserosa* was shown in the winter of 1911 at the St. Botolph Club in Boston; William Howe Downes, in *Dictionary of American Biography* (1930, rev. ed. 1959), s.v. "De Camp, Joseph Rodefer," notes that *La Penserosa* is one of De Camp's best-known figure pieces.

Exhibited:
Pennsylvania Academy of the Fine Arts, Philadelphia, 1908, *Exhibition of Paintings by Ten American Painters*, no. 24; St. Botolph Club, Boston, 1911; St. Botolph Club, Boston, 1924, *Memorial Exhibition of the Work of Joseph Rodefer De Camp*, no. 32, *Il Pensieroso*, possibly this work, in the estate of the artist.

Ex coll.:
Estate of the artist; Alexander Moffat, Manchester, Massachusetts; Marine Arts Gallery, Salem, Massachusetts, 1979; Dr. and Mrs. John J. McDonough, Youngstown, Ohio.

La Penserosa
c. 1904-08

oil on canvas
24 x 21 in. (61 x 53.3 cm.)
Signed, lower left: Joseph-De-Camp

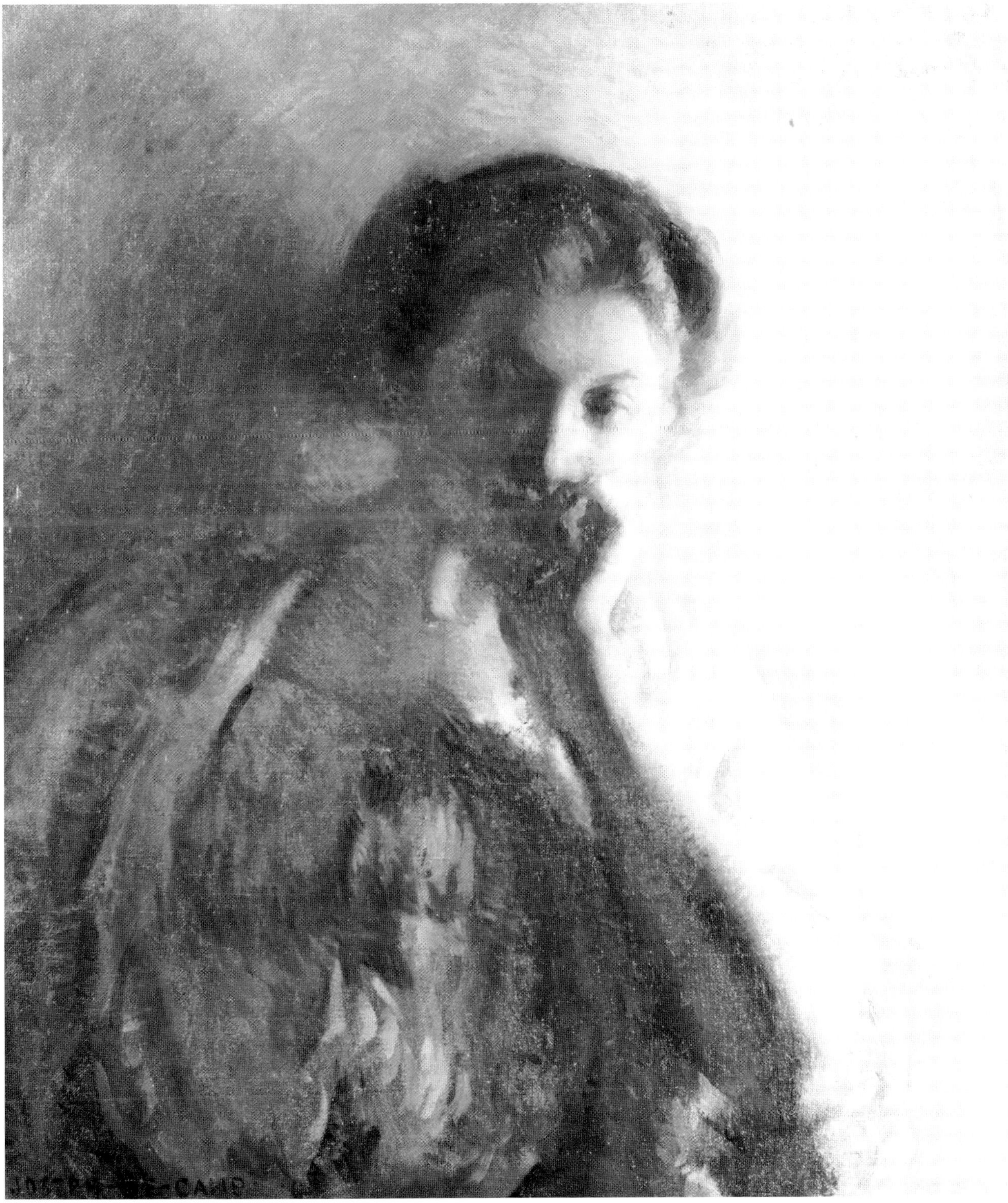

John Joseph Enneking
(1838-1916)

Enneking's trips to Europe between 1872 and 1876 exposed him to the latest trends in French painting and predisposed him to accept Impressionism. Back in the United States, however, he transformed this predisposition into a style that is difficult to define. Ralph Davol, a well-known Boston critic, characterized it in the following terms: "His Impressionism was never a matter of vivid greens and violets, yellow lights and purple shadows; nor was he of that 'cult of the innocent eye,' the pleinairists, who held that fleeting impressions should be instantaneously imprisoned and a picture completed on the spot. . . . He divided tones into their primary elements and obtained color vibrations by laying on fresh paint in gentle, juicy pounces with a narrow brush, carefully tucking in the edges of his strokes to preserve a delicate, volatile play of light. . . . His range of values was narrow—the result of shortening up deep shadows more than of subduing highlights" (Ralph Davol, "The Work of John J. Enneking," *American Magazine of Art* 8 [June 1917], pp. 320-325).

In this unusual still-life work possessing much in common with the composition of Twachtman's contemporary garden still-lifes (*Meadow Flowers*, c. 1890-1900, The Brooklyn Museum; *In the Greenhouse*, c. 1890-1902, North Carolina Museum of Art), the rich, pure colors preferred by Enneking and the individuality of his technique combine to produce a work that at once appears Impressionist and academic. It was probably begun outdoors in the garden of his summer house in North Newry, Maine, and completed in his studio, as was his usual practice.

Ex coll.:
Sale, Sotheby Parke-Bernet, Inc., New York, October 25, 1979, no. 127; Dr. and Mrs. John J. McDonough, Youngstown, Ohio.

Flowers in a Garden
1897

oil on canvas
30 x 22 in. (76.2 x 55.9 cm.)
Signed and dated, lower right: Enneking 97

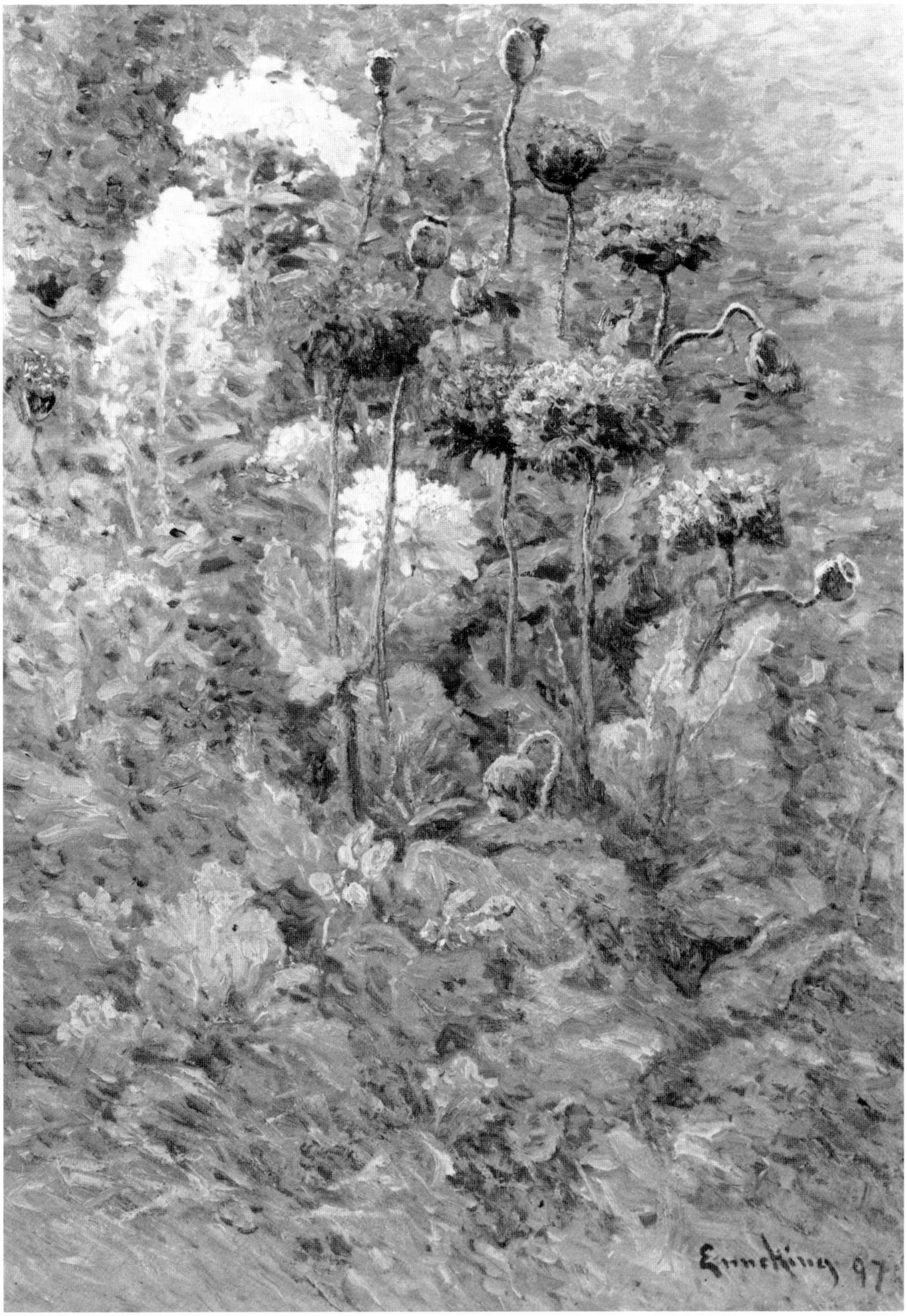

Frederick Carl Frieseke (1874-1939)

In an interview with the painter and writer Clara MacChesney, published in 1914, Frieseke stated: "it is sunshine, flowers in sunshine; girls in sunshine; the nude in sunshine, which I have been principally interested in for eight years, and if I could only reproduce it exactly as I see it I would be satisfied" (Clara T. MacChesney, *The New York Times*, June 7, 1914). These interests gained him a large reputation in Europe and America; in this country, however, Frieseke's flowers and girls sold well but not his nudes. This caused him some difficulties with his American dealer, William Macbeth, but Frieseke remained committed to painting the pictures of nudes on which his reputation in Europe largely rested. According to him, it was for this reason that he lived and worked in France: "I stay here because I am more free and there are not the Puritanical restrictions which prevail in America. Not only can I paint a nude here out of doors, but I can have a greater choice of subjects. As there are so few conventionalities in France, an artist can paint what he wishes. I can paint a nude in my garden or down by the fish pond and not be run out of town" (MacChesney, 1914).

Although *Nude on Beach* is not dated, it appears to represent the same nude model who appears in Frieseke's *Autumn* (1914, Museo d'Arte Moderna, Venice) and must have been executed about the same time. Another related work, featuring the same beach scene, model, parasol, and square dimensions, is *Girl in Blue* (unlocated, ill. in Telfair Academy of Arts and Sciences, 1974, p. 17). Unfortunately, this work is not dated.

Frieseke resided at Giverny in a house previously owned by Theodore Robinson and adjacent to Monet's property. It was not Monet's style that greatly influenced him, however, but that of the Postimpressionists Bonnard and Vuillard. In painting the female nude, as this painting bears out, he also owed much to Renoir.

References:
Antiques 106 (December 1974), p. 910, ill. in advertisement; *Art News* 74 (February 1975), ill. in color, p. 84; Hirschl and Adler Galleries, Inc., New York, *American Paintings, 1876-1963* (1975), p. 12, ill.

Exhibited:
Telfair Academy of Arts and Sciences, Savannah, Georgia, traveling exhibition, 1974-75, *Frederick Frieseke, 1874-1939*, not in cat.

Ex coll.:
Estate of Alexander Hamilton; Peterson Galleries, Los Angeles, 1978; Dr. and Mrs. John J. McDonough, Youngstown, Ohio.

Nude on Beach
c. 1915

oil on canvas
32½ x 32½ in. (82.6 x 82.6 cm.)
Signed, lower left: F. C. Frieseke.

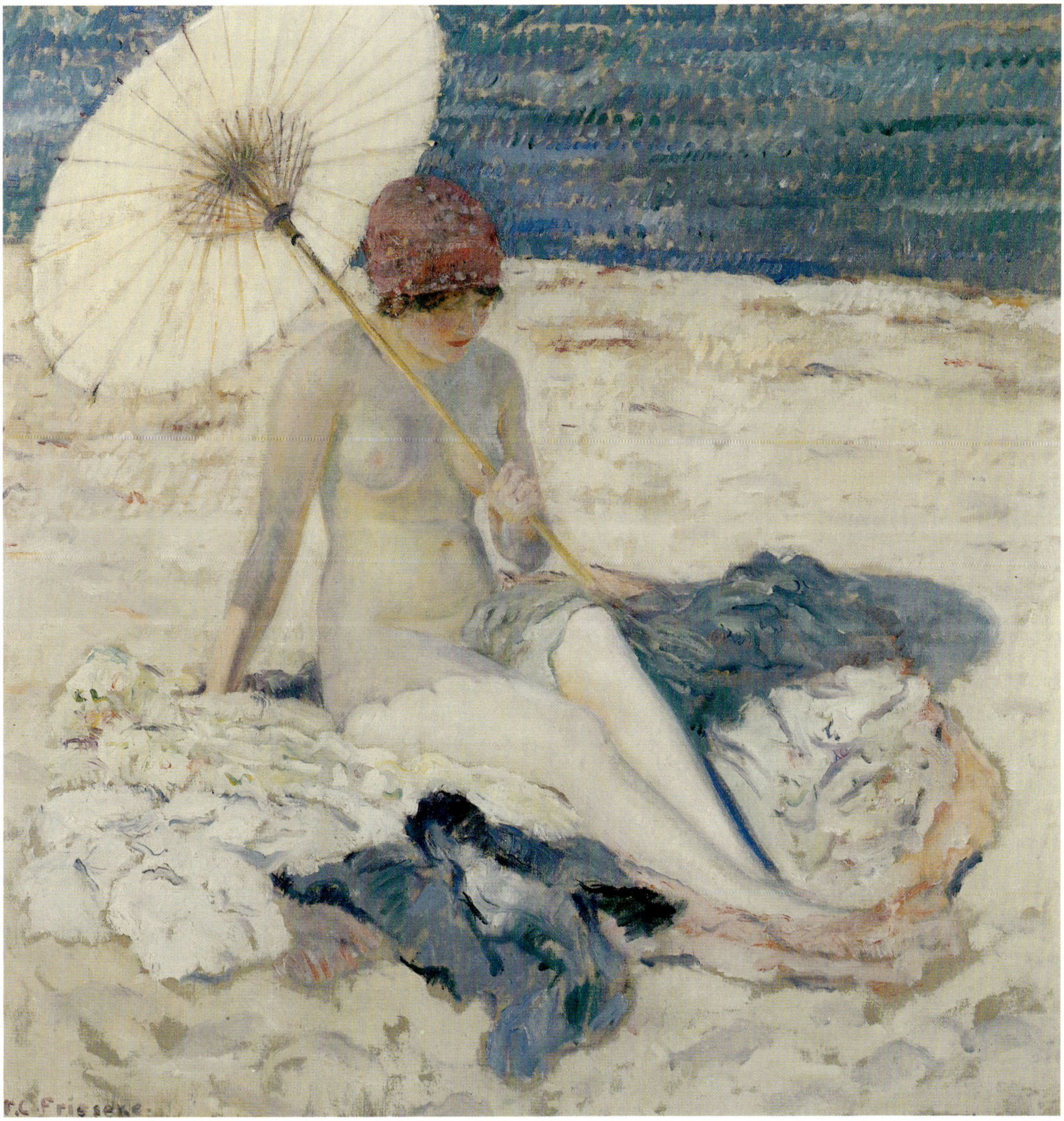

Arthur Clifton Goodwin (1864-1929)

Goodwin's atmospheric views of Boston were not too well-known during his lifetime. After his death, his work fell into even greater obscurity until 1946 when the respected art historian Lionello Venturi organized an exhibition of his landscapes and cityscapes at the Phillips Academy, Andover, Massachusetts, and at the Wildenstein Gallery in New York. Venturi thought highly of Goodwin's abilities: "he is self-taught; he is distinguished from all his contemporaries; his coloring is of the highest quality; he is a poet. He felt the pictorial value of the atmosphere of Boston as perhaps no other painter ever felt it. . . . He is the painter of Boston, as Utrillo is the painter of Montmartre, or Guardi of Venice" (Addison Gallery of American Art, Phillips Academy, Andover, Massachusetts, 1946, *Arthur Clifton Goodwin: A Selective Exhibition*, catalogue by L. Venturi, p. 5).

In this work, representing a view of Boston harbor on a cloudy winter day, Goodwin's ability at rendering atmospheric effects is much in evidence. The reflections of light in the water and the subtle variations of color and brushwork in the sky are handled in a typically Goodwinesque and highly individual manner. For most of his adult life, Goodwin was an alcoholic. Frequently, during bouts of heavy drinking, he retired to the wharves and docks of Boston where he had many friends among the longshoremen. The scene depicted here was probably very familiar to him and may well have had special meaning for him.

Exhibited:
Museum of Fine Arts, Boston, 1974, A.C. *Goodwin, 1864-1929*, no. 20, lent by Roye Levin.

Ex coll.:
Roye Levin, Boston; sale, Richard A. Bourne Company, Inc., Hyannis, Massachusetts, August 15, 1978, no. 116; Dr. and Mrs. John J. McDonough, Youngstown, Ohio.

The Mystic River Docks
c. 1915

oil on canvas
21 x 27 in. (53.3 x 68.6 cm.)
Signed, lower right: A.C. Goodwin

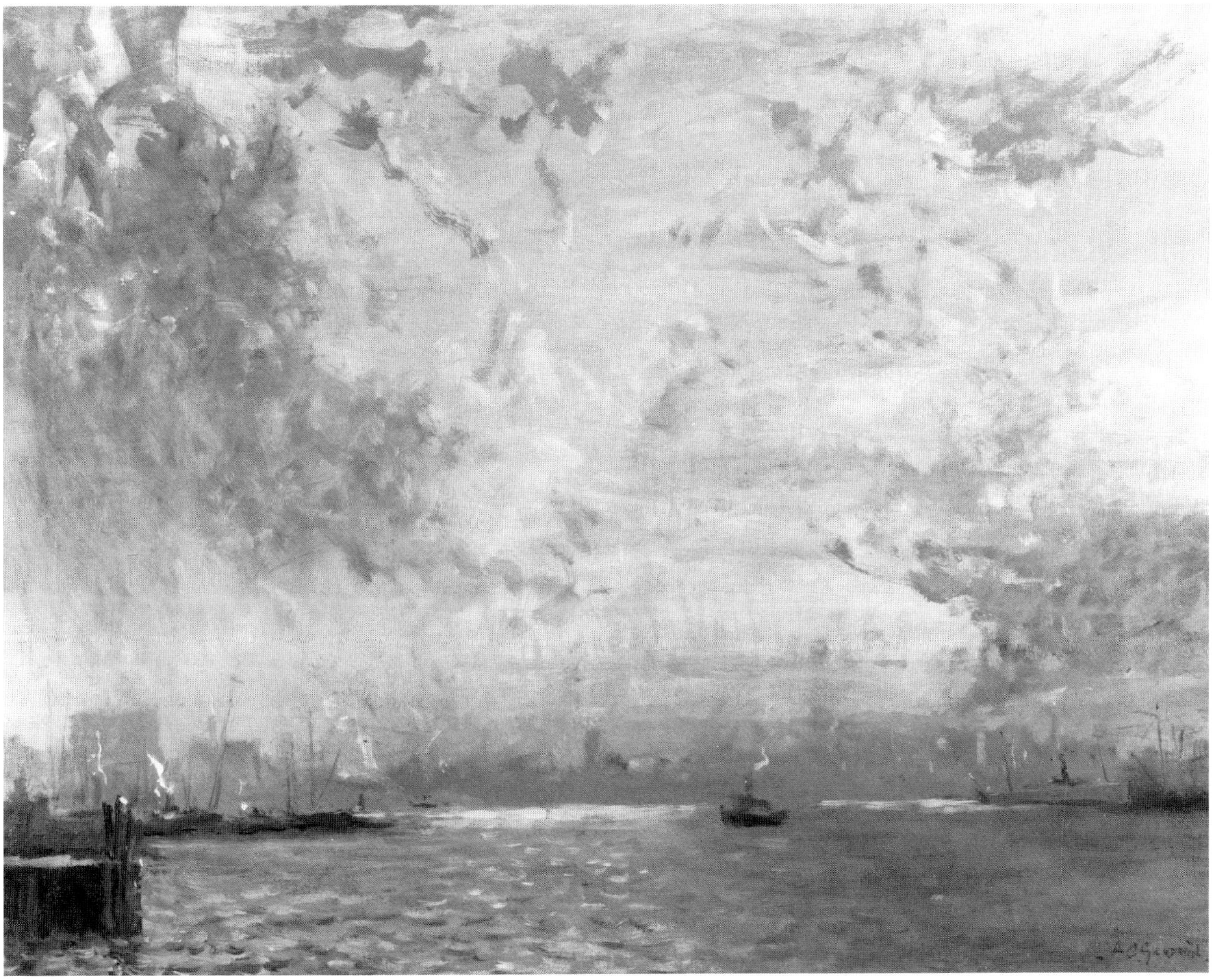

Childe Hassam
(1859-1935)

Childe Hassam first visited the fishing port of Gloucester, Massachusetts, in 1890. In subsequent years he returned many times, usually staying at a cottage that formed part of the Hawthorne Inn complex in East Gloucester. It was on Banner Hill, not far from this artists' resort, that Hassam painted this view of the harbor and town of Gloucester. By this time his Impressionist style had matured, as can be seen in the broken brushwork that captures the general effect of sparkling sunlight in the painting. Still, his representation of the physical features of the town in this work is a highly realistic one. To the right of the City Hall clocktower in the center of the painting is the spire of the First Baptist Church; further to the right, that of the Catholic Church of St. Ann's. To the left of the City Hall the Unitarian Church is faintly visible. The body of water in front of these distant buildings is Gloucester's Inner Harbor. The central area is Rocky Neck, where the chimney of a power plant for the Marine Railways provides a secular vertical accent. A number of boats are seen in the middleground, in a part of the harbor known as Smith's Cove. Most prominent in the view, however, is the house at 245 East Main Street, not far from where the painter John Sloan resided in the summers between 1914 and 1918.

Over the course of his career Hassam painted so many scenes in Gloucester that his vision of it as a bustling, picturesque harbor became an inseparable part of its appeal. Ernest Haskell noted this in 1922 when he wrote: "Before I had seen Hassam's pictures, [Gloucester] seemed a fishy little city, now as I pass through it I feel Hassam. The schooners beating in and out, the wharves, the sea, the sky, these belong to Hassam. Just as one cannot go to Venice and be very far from Whistler" (Ernest Haskell, in Nathaniel Pousette-Dart, *Childe Hassam* [1922], p. viii). In 1908 Hassam painted another view of Gloucester Harbor that is almost identical in composition and color to this one (Norton Gallery of Art, West Palm Beach, Florida).

G. S.

References:
Joseph Schoneman Galleries, Inc. New York, *Pictures on Exhibit* 8 (May 1946), pp. 21, 65; Steven Straw Company, Inc., Newburyport, Massachusetts, *American Selections 1977* (1977), unpaged, ill. in color; Donelson F. Hoopes, *Childe Hassam* (1979), p. 52.

Exhibited:
Joseph Schoneman Galleries, Inc., New York, 1946, *Paintings of All Schools*, no cat.; Milch Galleries, New York, 1947, *Thirty-Eight Years on 57th Street*, no. 9, as *Gloucester Harbor*, lent by Joseph Schoneman; Corcoran Gallery of Art, Washington, D.C., 1965, *Childe Hassam: A Retrospective Exhibition*, no. 28, as *Gloucester Harbor*, lent by Dr. and Mrs. Lazarus Marcus; Danforth Museum, Framingham, Massachusetts, 1978, *American Impressionist Painting*, unnumbered checklist.

Ex coll.:
Estate of the artist; Joseph Schoneman Galleries, Inc., New York; Dr. and Mrs. Lazarus Marcus, Brooklyn, New York; Terry deLapp, Los Angeles; Steven Straw Company, Inc., Newburyport, Massachusetts; Dr. and Mrs. John J. McDonough, Youngstown, Ohio.

Gloucester Harbor
1899

oil on canvas
24½ x 22½ in. (62.2 x 57.2 cm.)
Signed and dated, lower left: Childe Hassam 1899
Inscribed, on back: Gloucester Harbor/C.H./1899

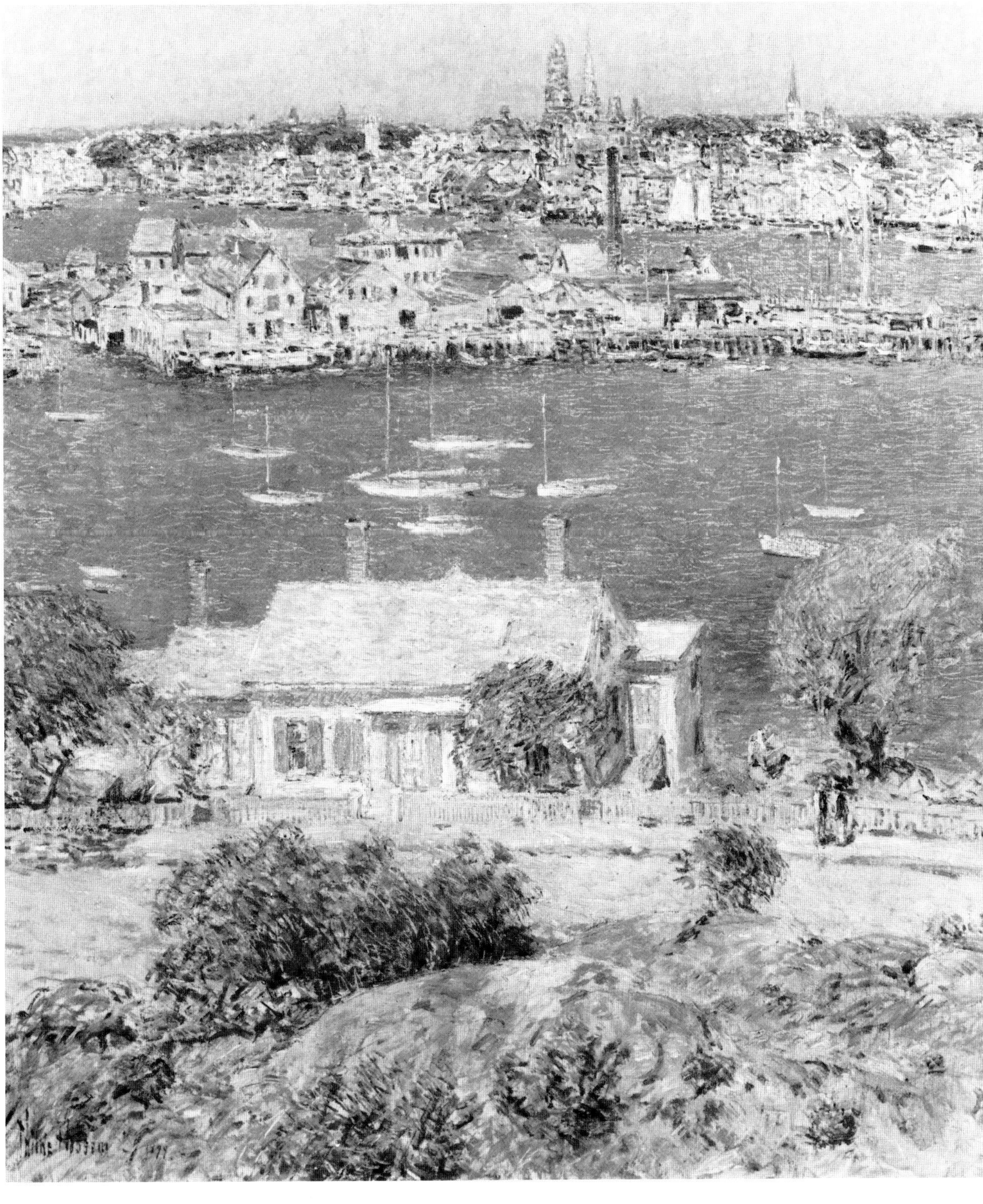

Robert Henri
(1865-1929)

Little Girl in Red was painted in the artists' colony of Woodstock, New York, during October of 1921. Although the Art Students' League, where Henri taught, was based in Woodstock during the summers, the artist took a leave of absence from his duties between June and October of that year in order to focus on painting. When he returned to New York in the fall, he had completed nearly one hundred works, including this portrait of Agnes Sleicher, one of his favorite Woodstock models.

This broadly painted, sympathetic study of a child is characteristic of Henri's later work. Although he painted masterful landscapes, Henri is best known as a portrait and figure painter who particularly liked to work with children. He viewed them as ideal, innocent beings unsullied by the evils of adulthood. In his book *The Art Spirit*, he wrote: "If you paint children you must have no patronizing attitude toward them. Whoever approaches a child without humility . . . wonderment and without infinite respect, misses in his judgment of what is before him, and loses an opportunity for a marvelous response. Children are greater than the grown man. All grown men have more experience, but only a very few retain the greatness that was theirs before the system of compromises began in their lives. . . . In the faces of children I have seen a look of wisdom and of kindness expressed with such ease and such certainty that I knew it was the expression of a whole race" (Robert Henri,*The Art Spirit*, [1923; ed. 1951], p. 186).

G. S.

References:
Robert Henri, *Notebook "L"*, ms. in possession of Chapellier Galleries, Inc., New York, gives title of painting, states when and where painted, and gives early exhibitions.

Exhibited:
Cincinnati Art Museum, Ohio, 1922, *Twenty-ninth Annual Exhibition of American Art*, no. 19; Carnegie Institute, Pittsburgh, 1923, *Paintings by Pittsburgh and Contemporary American Artists*, no. 13, as *Agnes in Red*; Memorial Art Gallery, Rochester, New York, 1926, *Irish and Spanish Portraits by Robert Henri*, no. 4.

Ex coll.:
Macbeth Gallery, Inc., New York, c. 1921; Dr. and Mrs. Harold Rifkin; Kraushaar Galleries, Inc., New York; sale, Sotheby Parke-Bernet, Inc., New York, April 20, 1979, no. 176; Dr. and Mrs. John J. McDonough, Youngstown, Ohio.

Little Girl in Red
1921

oil on canvas
24 x 20 in. (61 x 50.8 cm.)
Signed, lower right: Robert Henri
Signed, titled, and numbered, on back: Robert Henri/Little Girl in Red/178
L

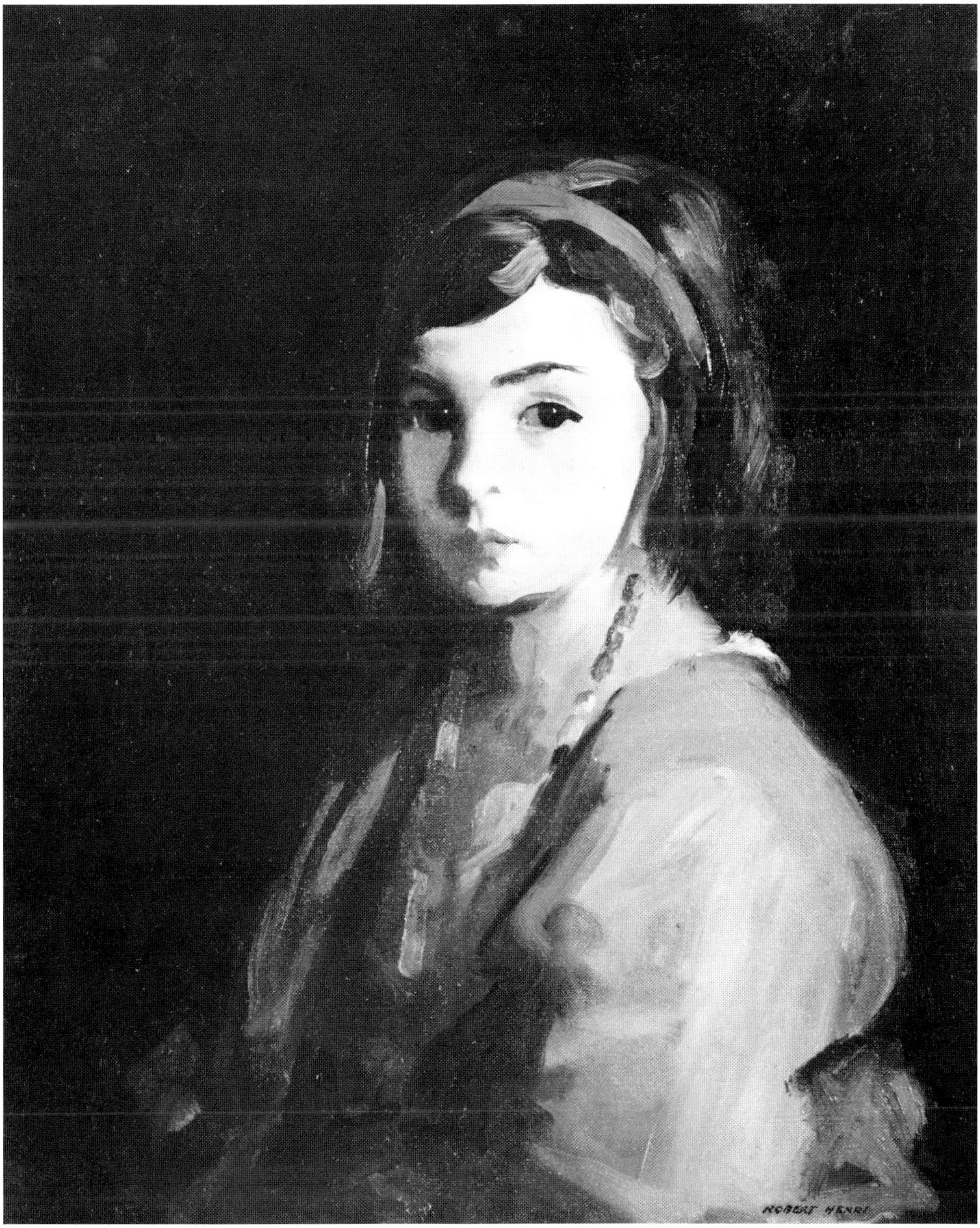

Robert Henri
(1865-1929)

Skipper Mick is a portrait of Jimmie Michael Macnamara who was painted by Henri in Ireland on October 20, 1924. Wishing to paint a wide variety of human types, Henri traveled in Europe and the United States almost every summer. His first of many trips to the remote Achill Island off the western coast of Ireland in 1913 provided Henri with a wide range of appealing subjects: majestic landscapes, old villages, and picturesque people. He eventually purchased a house there.

During his journeys abroad Henri painted dozens of children. *Skipper Mick* is a particularly fine example of his Irish portraits. With broad slashing brushstrokes in the tradition of Hals and Manet, Henri captured the vitality, dignity, and what he termed the "tremendous activity of a boy sitting still" (Robert Henri, *The Art Spirit* [1923, ed. 1951], p. 195). As was his usual practice, he probably finished the work in one sitting. Henri believed that fast work permitted the artist to represent fleeting gestures that revealed essential elements of character. Here, the child's hand stuffed in his pocket is such a gesture and projects an air of savvy and self-assurance that is also confirmed by his intensely alert glance.

International in his outlook, Henri painted children of other races and nationalities as individual "symbols of greatness" whose humanity he saw as transcending all institutional boundaries: "Every nation in the world in spite of itself, produces the occasional individual that . . . expresses . . . something of the dignity of life, the humor, the humanity, the kindness . . . that will rescue the race and the nation" (*The Art Spirit*, pp. 111-112).

G. S.

References:
Robert Henri, *Notebook "M"*, ms. in possession of Chapellier Galleries, Inc., New York, p. 193, gives title and states when painted; Macbeth Gallery, Inc., New York, *Art Notes*, No. 81 (April 1925), p. 1427; *Arts & Decoration* 23 (October 1925), ill. in color on cover; *Arts & Decoration* 33 (September 1930), ill. in color facing p. 49.

Exhibited:
Macbeth Gallery, Inc., New York, 1925, *Recent Paintings by Robert Henri, N.A.*; Metropolitan Museum of Art, New York, 1931, *Memorial Exhibition of the Works of Robert Henri*, no. 73.

Ex coll.:
Macbeth Gallery, Inc., New York, 1924; Mr. and Mrs. Carll Tucker, New York, 1925; their brother-in-law, Francis P. Garvan, New York, from 1929; his wife, Mabel Brady Garvan, New York, until 1980; sale, Sotheby Parke-Bernet, Inc., New York, April 25, 1980, no. 120; Dr. and Mrs. John J. McDonough, Youngstown, Ohio.

Skipper Mick
1924

oil on canvas
24 x 20 in. (61 x 50.8 cm.)
Signed, lower right: Robert Henri
Signed, titled, and numbered, on back: Robert Henri/Skipper Mick/193
M

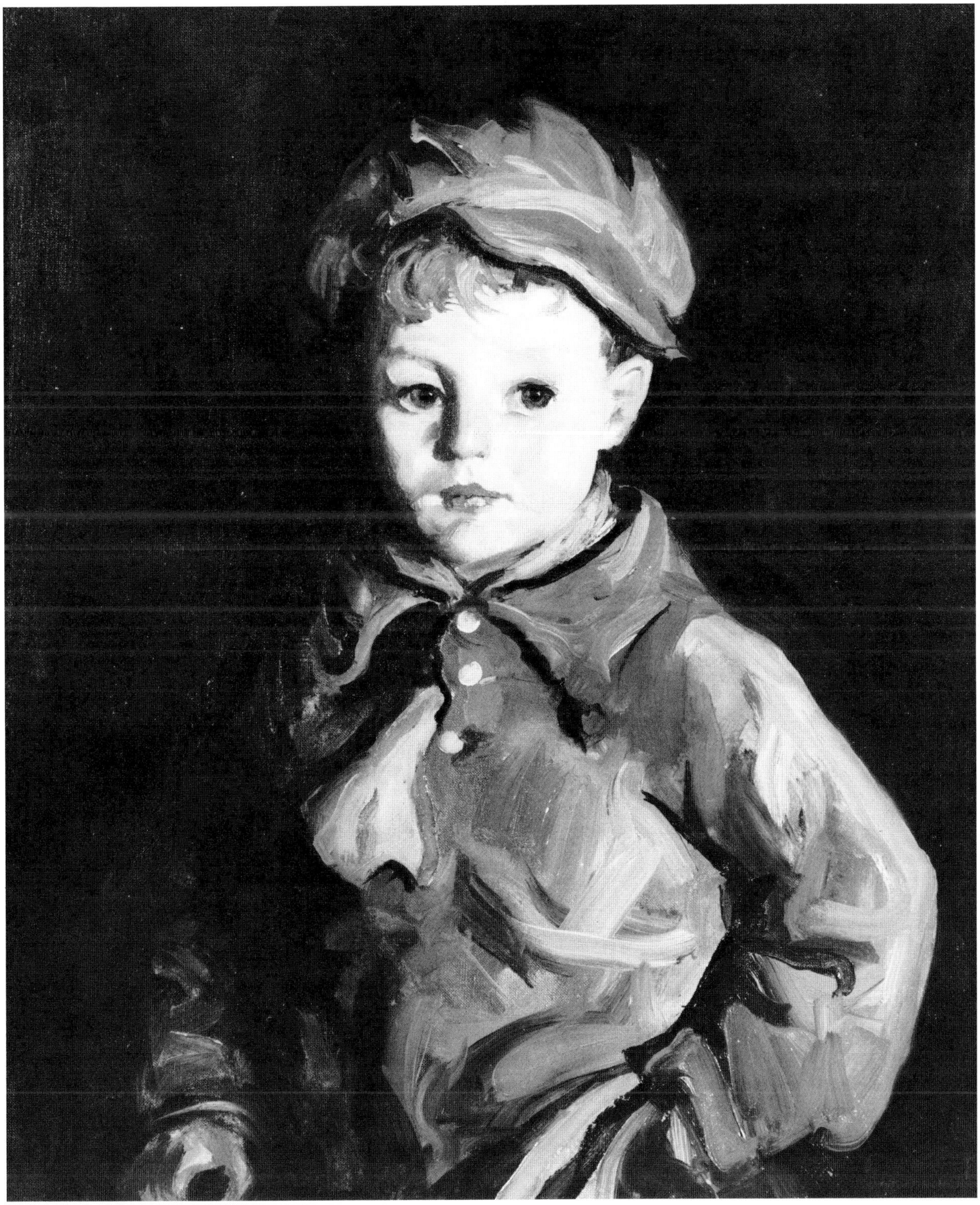

William H. Holmes
(1846-1933)

Holmes's artistic abilities gained him entry into the fields of geology, ethnology, and archaeology to which he devoted his professional life. He never gave up painting altogether, however, and he especially did not give up watercolor painting, which he seems to have pursued as a leisure-time activity. His watercolors were frequently exhibited at the Washington Water Color Club and won him prizes in 1900 and 1902. The largest public collection of them is now at the National Museum of American Art in Washington, D.C., the successor institution of the National Gallery of Art, of which Holmes was director.

Although it is not dated, *Girl Sitting on a Hillside* may be assigned to about 1900 on the basis of the girl's costume as well as of its style. Holmes seems to have produced his best watercolors about this time, when he also appears to have been influenced by the works of Winslow Homer in that medium.

Ex coll.:
Hirschl and Adler Galleries, Inc., New York, 1977; Steven Straw Company, Inc., Newburyport, Massachusetts, 1978; Dr. and Mrs. John J. McDonough, Youngstown, Ohio.

Girl Sitting on a Hillside
c. 1900

watercolor on paper
14½ x 21¼ in. (36.8 x 54 cm.)
Signed, lower left in artist's monogram: W.H.

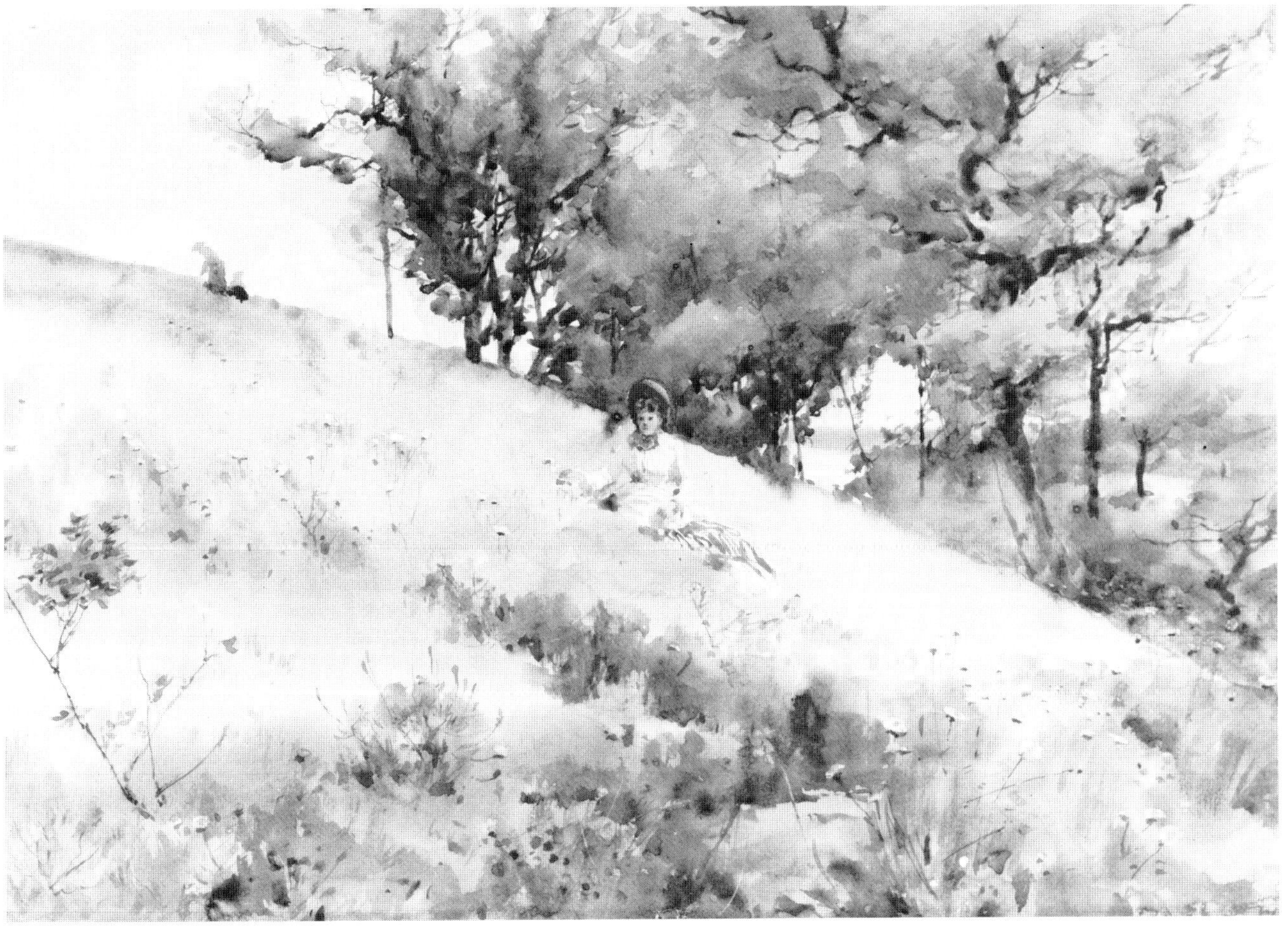

Walter Koeniger
(1881-1943)

In 1925 G. Frank Muller published what seems to be the only article on Koeniger ever to appear in an American publication of any importance. Muller characterized him as a "painter of snow" and noted of his style: " Koeniger's vision is not photographic; he works in broad strokes, never small or stilted, capturing the subtle relation of tones in large synthetic values of fresh, luminous, glowing color. His aim is to catch the spirit of nature, not to copy her slavishly" (G. Frank Muller, "Koeniger – Painter of Snow," *International Studio* 81 [June 1925], p. 214). Referring to the pictures, generally square, of brooks and streams winding their way through snow-covered woods, Muller wrote: "[Koeniger] is deeply concerned with the moods of nature; the soft gradations of violet, purple, deep blue, and heliotrope of the deep snow; with the emerald sky, the lazy brooks, and the silver, glistening branches of the stately pines" (p. 214). This theme, treated in the colors described by Muller, occupied him throughout the 1920s and 30s. Variations in the time of day represented, in the windings of the stream, or in the shape of the leafless tree limbs, distinguish these works one from the other, but in essence Koeniger painted the same painting over and over: a solitary ice-bound stream flowing toward the viewer through a snow-clad forest that shows no sign of human presence.

Koeniger received his training in painting in Germany, but it is clear from his works that the greatest influences upon his mature art were the snow landscapes of Gardner Symons and Walter Schofield, which were highly publicized in the 1910s and 20s and established a certain fashion for this type of picture.

Ex coll.:
Sale, Sotheby Parke-Bernet, Inc., New York, April 15, 1970, no. 225; Dr. and Mrs. John J. McDonough, Youngstown, Ohio.

Winter Landscape
c. 1925

oil on canvas
32 x 32 in. (81.3 x 81.3 cm.)
Signed, lower right: W. Koeniger

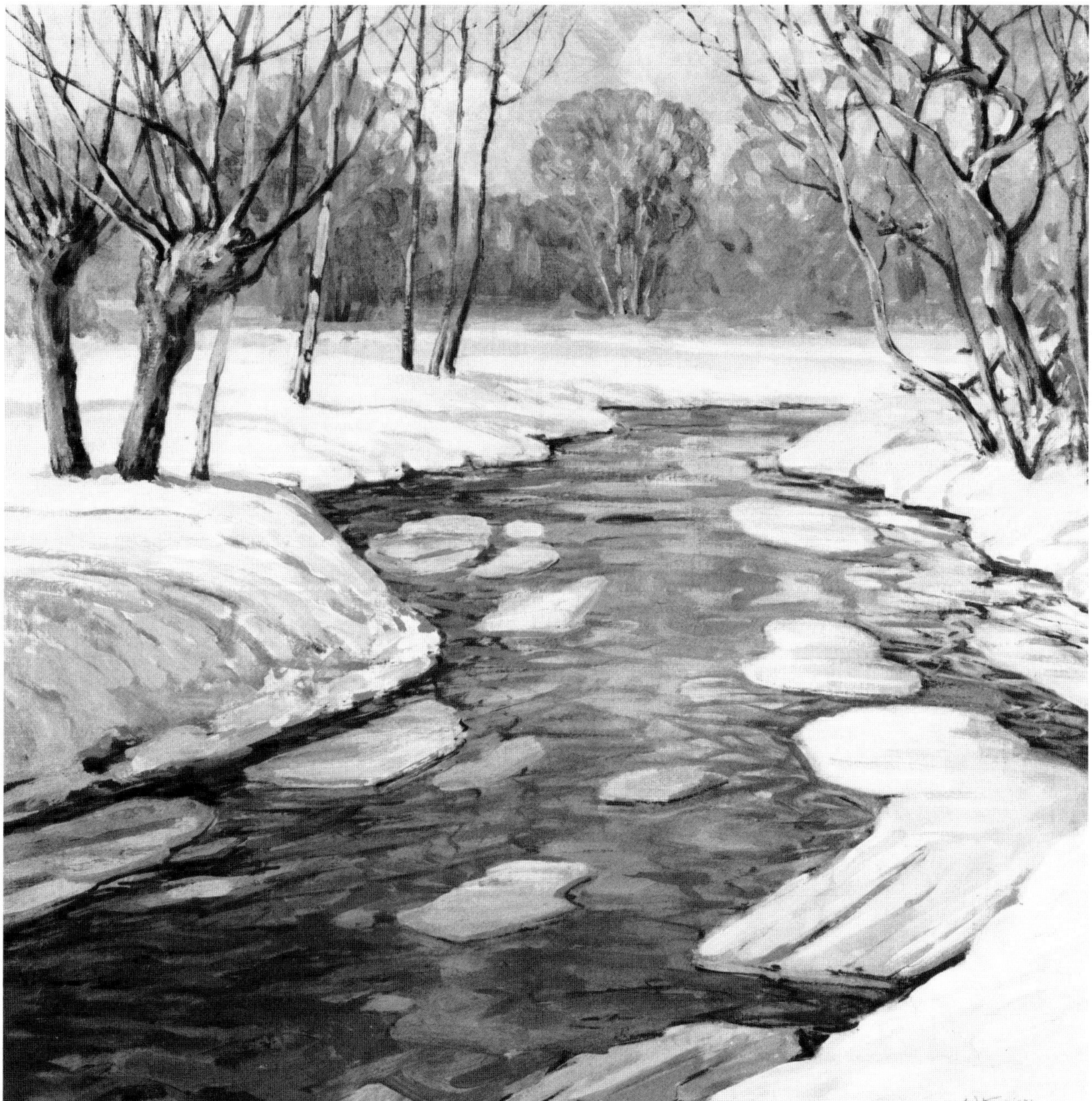

Ernest Lawson
(1873-1939)

In 1898 Ernest Lawson moved to 155th Street in New York City, then part of a sparsely inhabited neighborhood. Until about 1906 he painted mostly scenes in and around this area, still known as Washington Heights. It was at this time that his individual style, largely influenced by the paintings of Pissarro and Cézanne he had seen in France, began to emerge. It was not a style meant to be pretty or decorative, but rather one emphasizing bluntness, heavily impastoed execution, and sparkling, but not necessarily accurate, color. At first his works were dismissed as simply ugly, but after 1904, when the artist won the Silver Medal at the St. Louis International Exposition, they met with ever-increasing acclaim.

Although it is not dated, the completion of *Morningside Heights* must have taken place about 1902 or 1903 when the Cathedral of St. John the Divine, a transept arch of which is seen in the upper left corner, was beginning to be built. It depicts Morningside Park in the neighborhood of 112th Street as well as the large apartment buildings that had recently been erected on Broadway and on Amsterdam Avenue near Columbia University. The perspective is from a high point near the park and recalls Pissarro's use of this device in a number of his views of Paris. A large and ambitious work, it is not painted in the heavy manner Lawson increasingly adopted but still retains a good deal of what Duncan Phillips called Lawson's "earlier lyric impressionism" (Duncan Phillips, *A Collection in the Making* [1926], p. 57).

Exhibited:
A.C.A. Heritage Gallery, Inc., New York, 1967, *Ernest Lawson, 1873-1939*, no. 1, ill. in color on cover; National Academy of Design, New York, 1975, *A Century and a Half of American Art*, p. 88; A.C.A. Galleries, Inc., New York, 1976, *Ernest Lawson Retrospective*, exhibition catalogue by Dennis Anderson, no. 5, ill. p. 21.

Ex coll.:
Daniel Gallery, Inc., New York, about 1923; Grantland Rice, New York; A.C.A. Heritage Gallery, Inc., New York, 1967; unidentified private collection; A.C.A. Galleries, Inc., New York; George Arden, New York, 1971; sale, Sotheby Parke-Bernet, Inc., New York, April 25, 1980, no. 119A; Dr. and Mrs. John J. McDonough, Youngstown, Ohio.

Morningside Heights
c. 1902-03

oil on canvas
34½ x 40½ in. (87.6 x 102.9 cm.)
Signed, lower right: E. Lawson

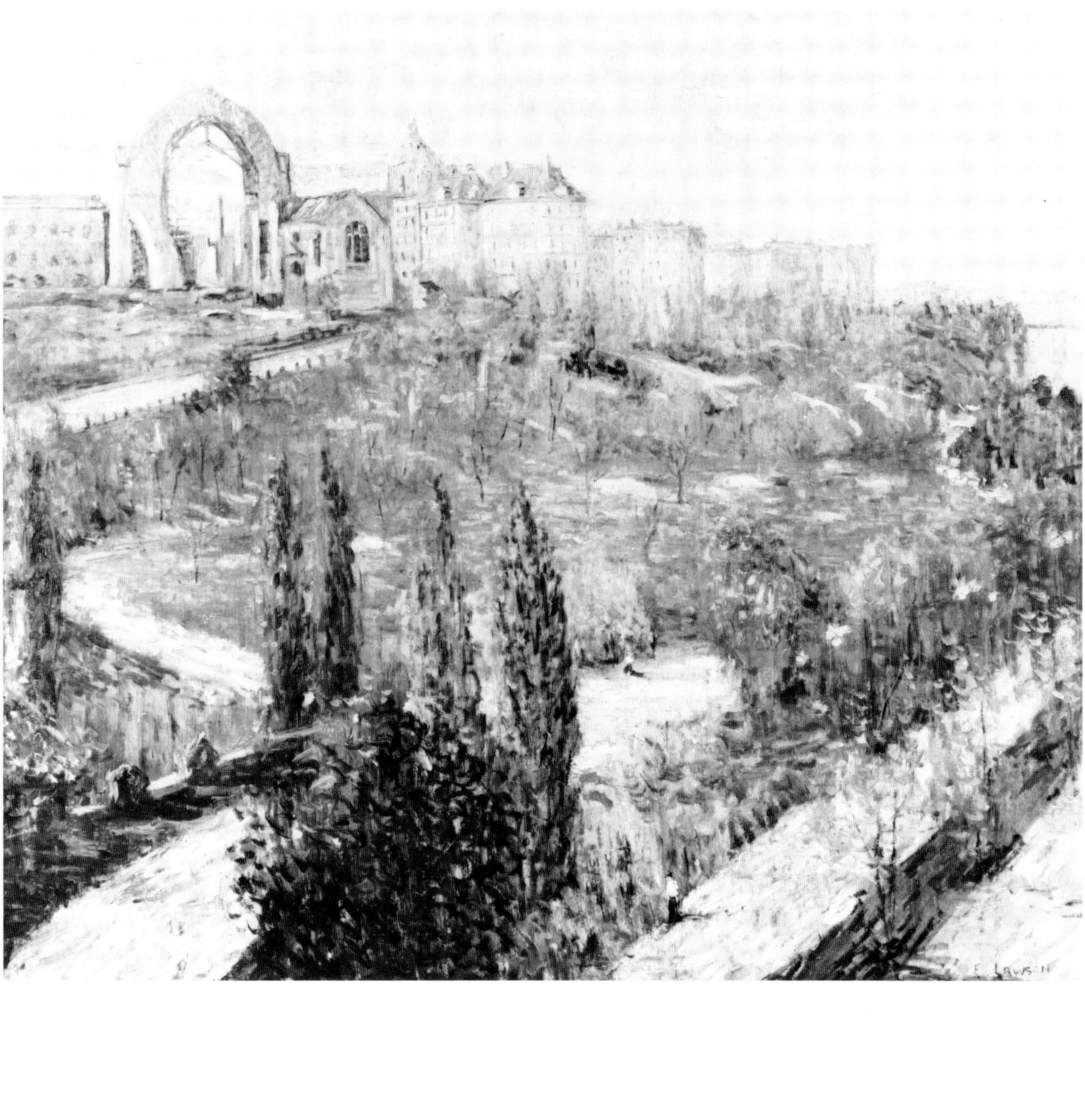

Hayley Lever
(1876-1958)

For most of his career, Lever was viewed as a marine painter. His winning the Carnegie Prize at the National Academy of Design in 1914 with one of his rather stylized seascapes was thought in many quarters to have been an unexpectedly progressive step by that institution. It received a good deal of attention in artistic circles at the time and firmly established Lever's reputation as a painter of the sea. The artist was interested in other subjects, however, and painted landscapes and cityscapes throughout his life.

Although the precise date of execution of this work is not known, it is certain that it was painted between the time of Lever's arrival in America and about 1922, when pictures depicting similar views, perhaps including this one, were exhibited at the Macbeth Gallery in New York. Showing a view of the Manhattan business district from the neighborhood of the Lackawanna Railroad station in Hoboken, New Jersey, *Lower Manhattan* is executed in the painterly, layer-like manner of Lever's early American works and may well date from 1912 or 1913. It presents New York as a somewhat unreal and ghostly conglomeration of buildings rising sharply from the water's edge and standing in clear contrast to the colorful and more comprehensible scenes on the Hudson River and on the New Jersey shore. This composition effectively conveys an image of Manhattan as being at once separate, monumental, fascinating, and fantasy-like, an image that is still presented to every traveler who approaches the city from this part of New Jersey.

Exhibited:
Macbeth Gallery, Inc., New York, 1922, *Paintings by Frederick C. Frieseke and Hayley Lever*, no. 23, as *Lower New York*, probably this work; no. 22, *From the Lackawanna* (unlocated, photograph in Artist Files, New York Public Library), depicts a similar view.

Ex coll.:
Macbeth Gallery, Inc., New York, 1922; Bernard Black Gallery, New York; Joan Patterson Roberts, New Canaan, Connecticut, until 1978; sale, Sotheby Parke-Bernet, Inc., New York, April 21, 1978, no. 66; Dr. and Mrs. John J. McDonough, Youngstown, Ohio.

Lower Manhattan
c. 1912-22

oil on canvas
25 x 30 in. (63.5 x 76.2 cm.)
Signed, lower left: Hayley Lever

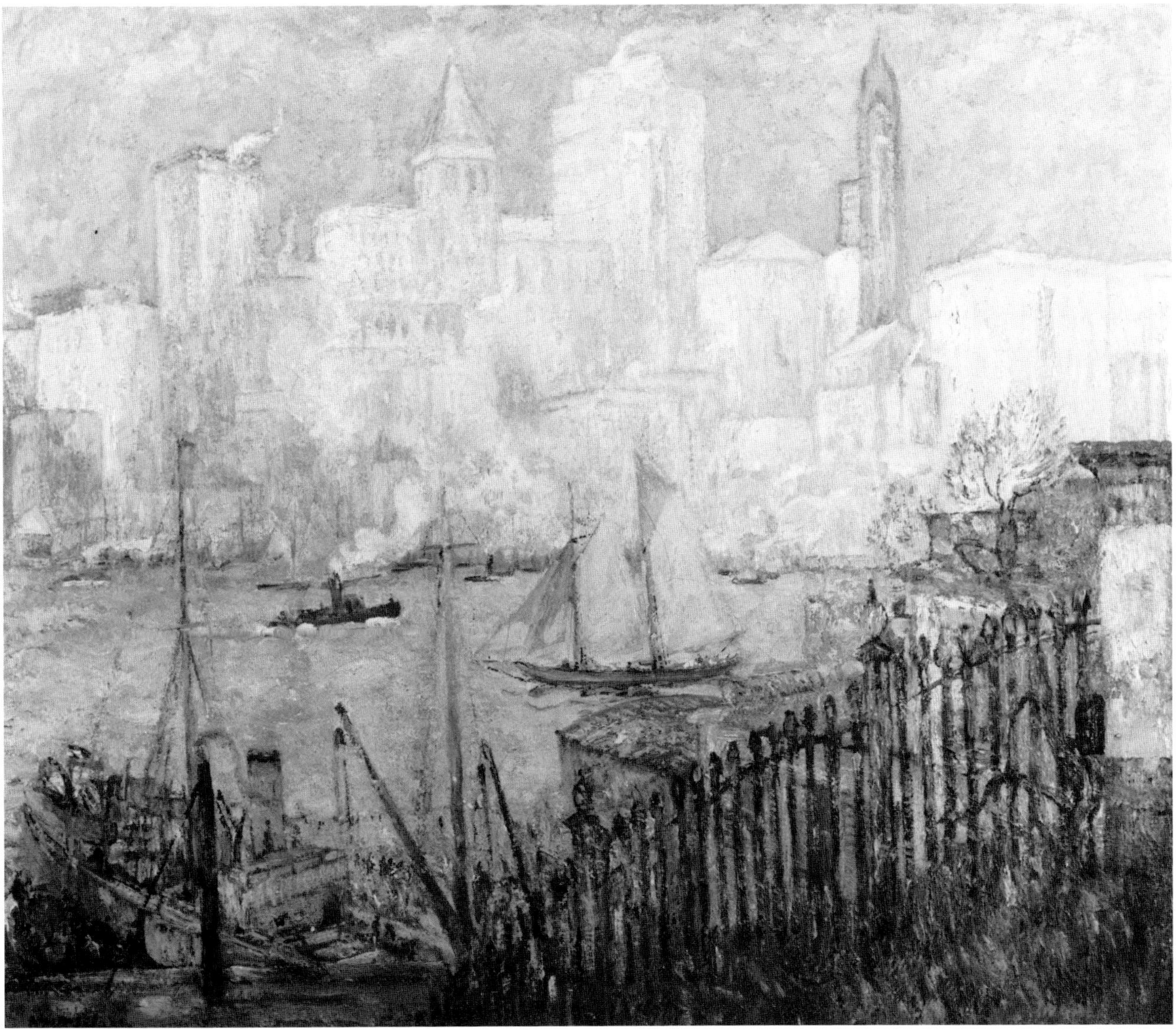

Willard Leroy Metcalf
(1858-1925)

Though he had been a founding member of the Ten American Painters in 1898, Metcalf's mature style did not crystallize until 1903 when, at the age of forty-five, he left New York and retired to Maine for a year. During this time he lived in near poverty with his parents – his father was on a meager Civil War veteran's pension of $8.50 a month – and did nothing but paint landscapes. Metcalf himself considered 1904 the year of his professional "renaissance," and the critics agreed. In 1904 an exhibition of his works at the Fishel, Adler and Schwartz Gallery, including many of his recent works, met with enormous success. Royal Cortissoz, a leading critic of the time, noted: "His Maine studies reflect a sympathy more alert and more penetrating than he was wont to disclose sometime ago and the exhibition was remarkable for nothing more than for its truth to the very soul of the American landscape as it is known in its most characteristic phases" (quoted in Teevan, 1925, p. 10). Henceforth, Metcalf's reputation as a landscape painter increased steadily until the time of his death when a newspaper obituary called him "the leading American landscape painter" (*The New York Times*, March 10, 1925).

Painted at this critical juncture in the artist's career, *Boothbay Harbor* is a masterpiece of composition and muted color. Cortissoz's remark that Metcalf "can give you a seemingly unstudied episode from the Maine coast in which the composition is nevertheless almost formal in the perfection of its balance" particularly applies to it (R. Cortissoz, *American Artists* [1923], p. 144). Its qualities were perceived in 1925 when Bernard Teevan in commenting upon Metcalf's progress wrote: "There was a time a few years since when I did not see how he could tune his instrument higher. This was when I knew canvases of the order of the 'Boothbay Harbor' " (Teevan, 1925, p. 10).

References:

Bernard Teevan, "A Painter's Renaissance," *International Studio* 82 (October 1925), pp. 3-11, gives Cortissoz citation and comments on this work on p. 10.

Ex coll.:

Milch Galleries, New York, c. 1925; sale, Parke-Bernet Galleries, New York, November 24, 1939, no. 41; W.H. Vanderpool; sale, Sotheby Parke-Bernet Galleries, Inc., New York, April 21, 1978, no. 80; Dr. and Mrs. John J. McDonough, Youngstown, Ohio.

Boothbay Harbor
1904

oil on canvas
26 x 29 in. (66 x 73.7 cm.)
Signed and dated, lower right: W. L. Metcalf '04

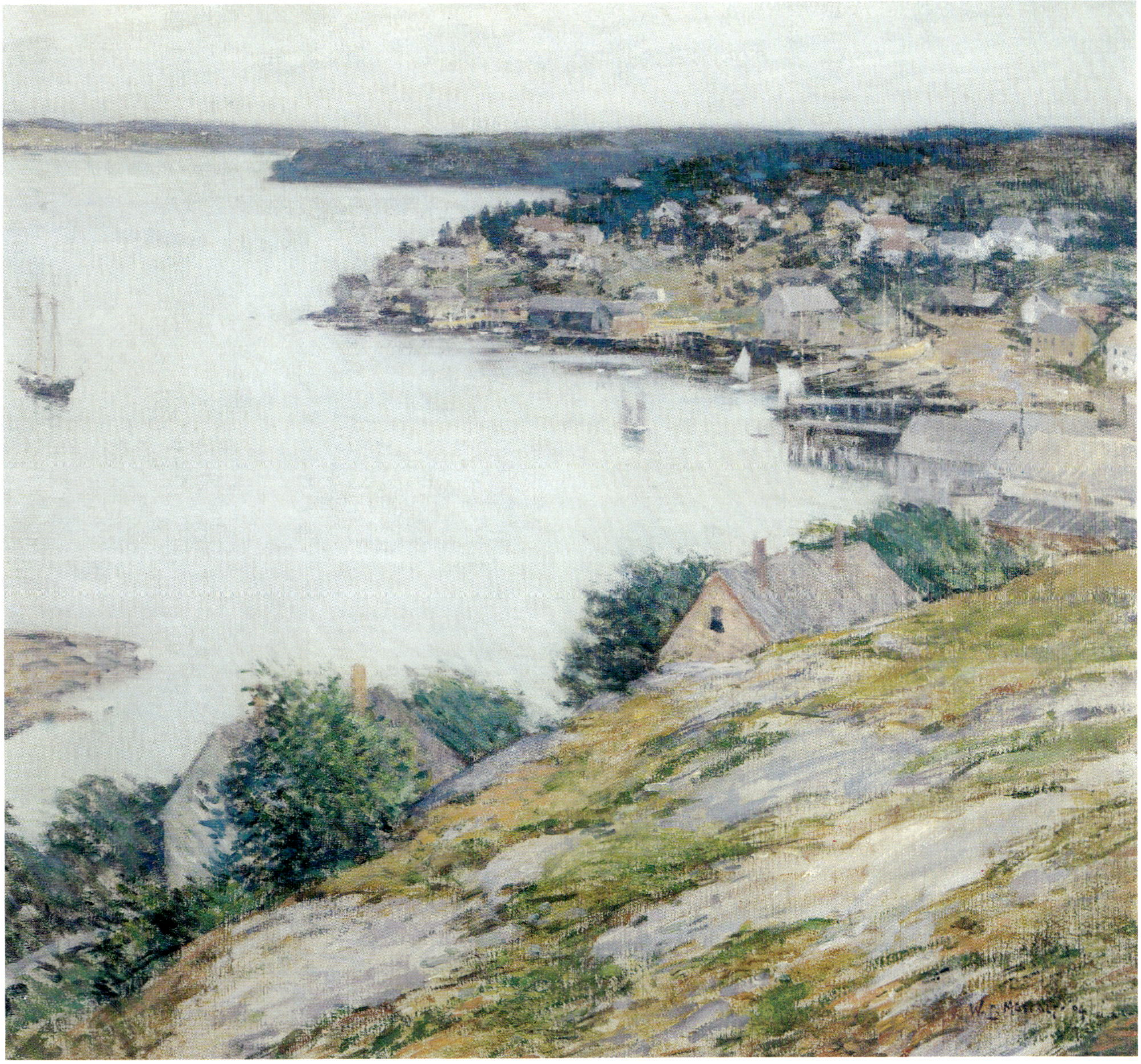

Richard Emil Miller
(1875-1943)

Because he lived in France for a good part of his life and because his works were invariably representations of women, Miller was frequently associated with Frieseke. Miller's mature style, however, did not develop from an early commitment to Impressionism but rather from the free-brushwork figural painting of Sargent, Giovanni Boldini, and Antonio Mancini. His debt to Impressionism is therefore in his color rather than in his technique, which consisted of defining the anatomical parts of his figures clearly and carefully and of surrounding them with draperies and accoutrements painted in a decorative patch-like fashion. These are in highly varied textures and give his works a particularly rich surface.

Miller's women are usually posed in a state of reverie in front of boudoir dressing tables, absorbed in themselves or looking at their jewelry. He frequently gave the same title to more than one painting, thus creating a certain confusion for students of his art. This work, for example, was purchased with the title *Lady at Her Vanity*, but in 1925 it was published by the Grand Central Art Galleries in New York, where Miller frequently exhibited, as *The Necklace*, also the title of a completely different Miller work purchased by the National Academy of Design in 1924. The same is true of two paintings called *The Sun Porch*, one exhibited at the 1920 Carnegie International and illustrated in its catalogue, and the other formerly in the collection of Carnegie Institute (1922, photograph in archives, Museum of Art, Carnegie Institute).

References:
Grand Central Art Galleries, New York, *Yearbook 1925*, no. 109, ill. as *The Necklace*, 26 x 28 in.

Exhibited:
Grand Central Art Galleries, New York, 1925, *Exhibition of Paintings and Sculpture Contributed by the Founders of the Gallery*, no cat.

Ex coll.:
Vose Galleries, Inc., Boston, 1978; Dr. and Mrs. John J. McDonough, Youngstown, Ohio.

The Necklace
c. 1920-25

oil on canvas
26 x 28 in. (66 x 71.1 cm.)
Signed, lower right: Miller

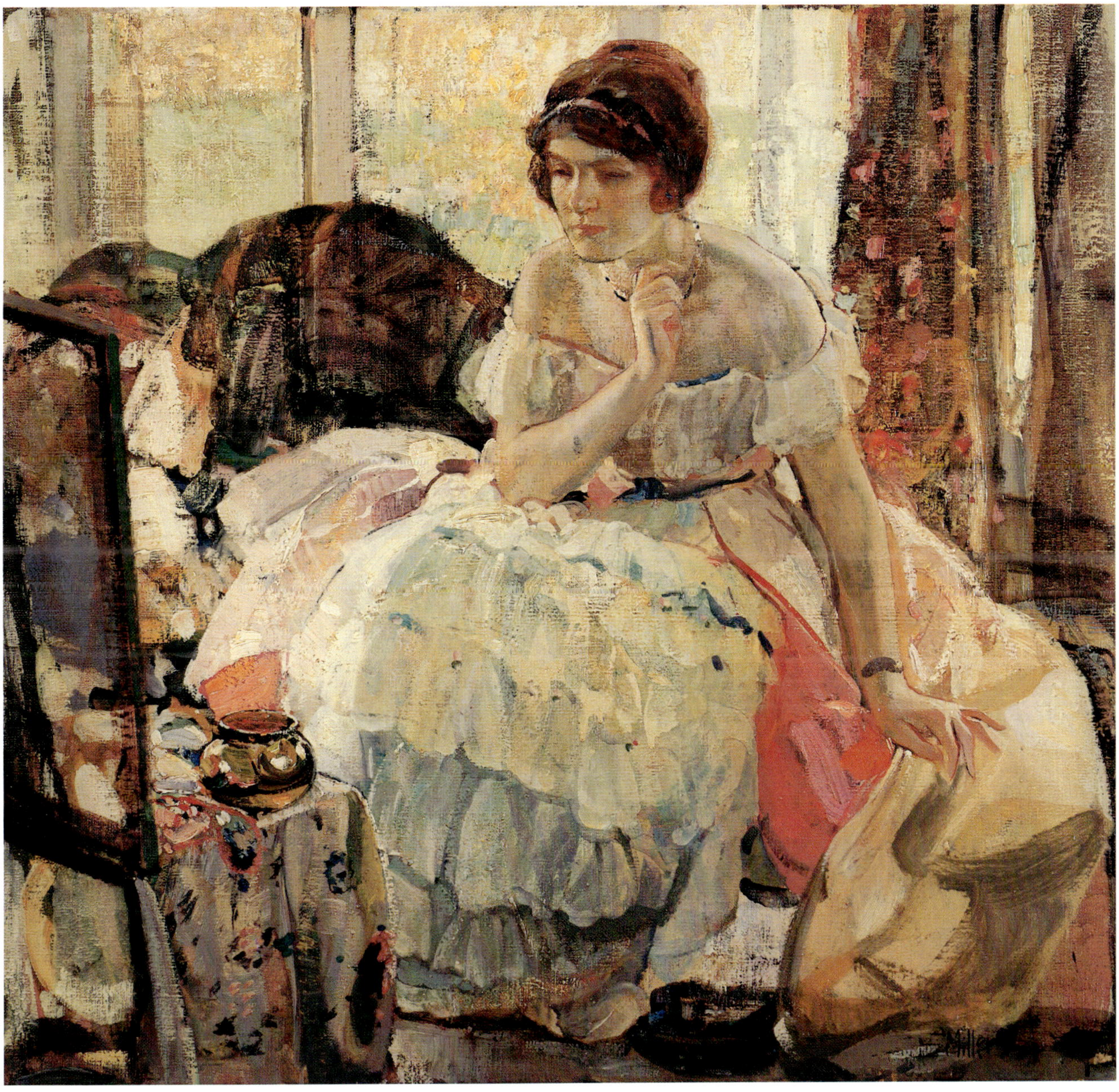

William McGregor Paxton (1869-1941)

The Sun Hat, also known as *My Wife, Elizabeth*, is a portrait of the artist's wife Elizabeth Okie Paxton. An artist in her own right, she specialized in still-life subjects and was a frequent exhibitor along with her husband at the annual exhibitions of contemporary American art held in Boston, Buffalo, Chicago, Pittsburgh, and Washington, D.C. Paxton met her at the Cowles Art School, after his return from Europe in 1893. They were engaged in the summer of 1896 and married in January 1899. Joseph Rodefer De Camp, Paxton's teacher and friend, reputedly acted as the matchmaker. She died in 1971.

Paxton frequently used his wife as a model in paintings of interiors intended as thematic works. However, in this case, it appears that he actually intended to paint a portrait of her. Certainly, Mrs. Paxton, who kept the work until her death, considered it as one. In addition, the scale of the figure, unusually large for Paxton, suggests this. Although it is not dated it may be assigned to about 1910 on the basis of a comparison of Mrs. Paxton's likeness here with that in the work titled *The Sisters* (private collection) executed in 1904. That painting depicts a slightly younger Mrs. Paxton with her sister Adele in an interior displaying pieces of furniture from the set to which the chair seen in *The Sun Hat* belongs. In *The Sisters* as well as in *The Sun Hat* the highlights of background objects are painted twice, according to Paxton's theory of "binocular vision." As Philip Leslie Hale explained it in an article published in 1909, this method was based on the premise that "upright lines behind or before the focusing point go double." Hale continued: "The joke of it is that he [Paxton] painted in this manner for years without anyone noticing what he was up to; they only perceived that his backgrounds had a remarkable quality of 'staying back' " (Philip Leslie Hale, "William McGregor Paxton," *International Studio* 39 [December 1909], p. xlviii).

References:
Patricia Jobe Pierce, letter to Dr. John J. McDonough, April 9, 1979, says "Wm. Paxton loved this painting and Mrs. Elizabeth Okie Paxton had it hanging in her apartment in the 1960's because she thought 'it looks so very much like me'."

Exhibited:
Pierce Galleries, Inc., Hingham, Massachusetts, 1977, *Boston Impressionists*, no cat.

Ex coll.:
The artist's wife, Elizabeth Okie Paxton, until 1971; Robert Douglas Hunter, Boston; Pierce Galleries, Inc., Hingham, Massachusetts, 1977; John P. McMorrow, Boston; sale, Barridoff Galleries, Inc., Portland, Maine, April 7, 1979, no. 28; Dr. and Mrs. John J. McDonough, Youngstown, Ohio.

The Sun Hat
c. 1910

oil on canvas mounted on board
34 x 24 in. (86.4 x 61 cm.)
Signed, upper left: Paxton

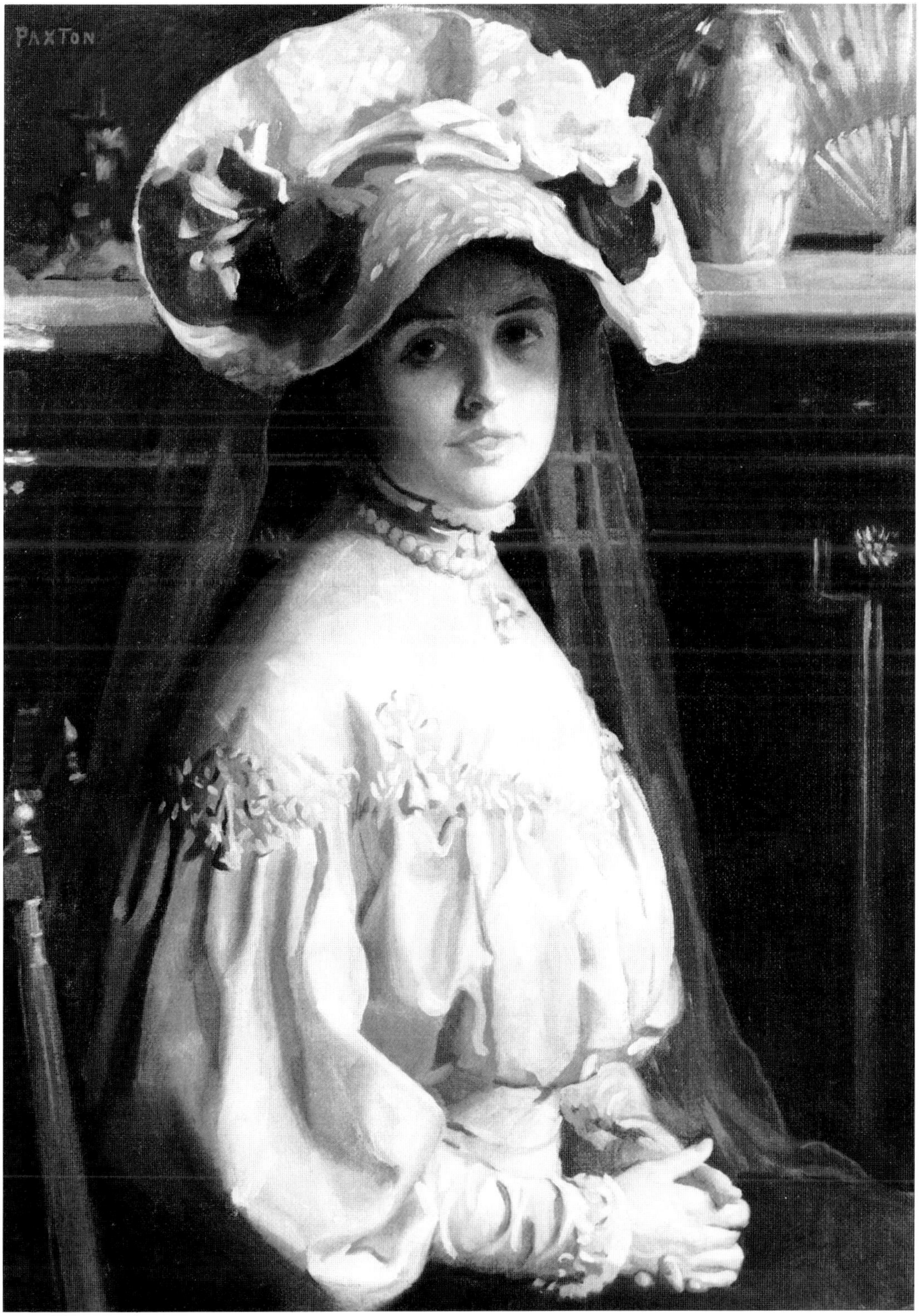

William McGregor Paxton
(1869-1941)

In a review of the 1911 exhibition of works by Boston artists held at the Museum of Fine Arts, the scene depicted here was described as follows: "This, a new canvas, is probably the best interior Mr. Paxton has made. It shows a delightful room, in which a young couple are seated at the breakfast table. The husband is deep in the morning newspaper, which hides all but a small part of his face from view; and that his absorption in the news of the day does not altogether please his better-half is quite evident from her pose and expression. She has turned half-way from the table, and is paying no attention to the tempting half of a grape-fruit or the dish of choice grapes before her place; in fact a domestic storm-signal may be said to be flying, though the man of the house does not notice it. A demure maid, in black, is just leaving the room, and her back says as plainly as words could express it: 'I know my business and this is none of it' " (*The Boston Transcript*, April 10, 1911).

It was with works of this type that Paxton captured the admiration of thousands of exhibition-goers in the years between 1910 and 1930. Repeatedly, they voted for his works to receive the so-called Popular Prizes which, at that time, were a regular feature of the major annual exhibitions of contemporary paintings. Like De Camp, Paxton was part of the Boston group of painters known as "Tarbellites," now usually referred to as the Boston School. Clearly influenced by Tarbell, Paxton went on to develop his own style of detailed realism, characterized by virtually invisible brushwork and muted, Vermeeresque, contrasts of light.

References:
The Boston Transcript, April 10, 1911; *The Boston Herald*, June 18, 1911, ill.; *Philadelphia Public Ledger*, February 4, 1912; *The Boston Transcript*, February 7, 1913; *Ladies' Home Journal* 30 (March 1913), ill. in color; Martin F. Krause, Jr., letter to Dr. John J. McDonough, December 12, 1978, gives bibliography and lists exhibitions.

Exhibited:
Museum of Fine Arts, Boston, 1911, *Works by Boston Artists*, no. 50; Worcester Art Museum, Worcester, Massachusetts, 1911, *14th Annual Exhibition of Oil Paintings by American Artists*, no. 43; Art Institute of Chicago, 1911, *24th Annual Exhibition of American Oil Paintings*, no. 273; Pennsylvania Academy of the Fine Arts, Philadelphia, 1912, *107th Annual Exhibition*, no. 149; Cincinnati Art Museum, Cincinnati, Ohio, 1912, *19th Annual Exhibition of American Art*, no. 33; Corcoran Gallery of Art, Washington, D.C., 1912-1913, *4th Exhibition of Oil Paintings by Contemporary American Artists*, no. 173; St. Botolph Club, Boston, 1913, *Paintings by William McGregor Paxton*, no. 5; Panama-Pacific International Exposition, San Francisco, 1915, no. 3771; The Rosenbach Company, Philadelphia, 1918, *Paintings by William M. Paxton*, no. 9; Indianapolis Museum of Art, Indianapolis, Indiana, traveling exhibition, 1978-1979, *William McGregor Paxton*, not in cat., exhibited in Springfield, Massachusetts only.

Ex coll.:
The artist; Mrs. Stuart Cook, Concord, Massachusetts; private collection, Lunenberg, Massachusetts; Vose Galleries, Inc., Boston, 1978; Dr. and Mrs. John J. McDonough, Youngstown, Ohio.

The Breakfast
1911

oil on canvas
28 x 34 in. (71.1 x 86.4 cm.)
Signed, lower right: Paxton - 1911

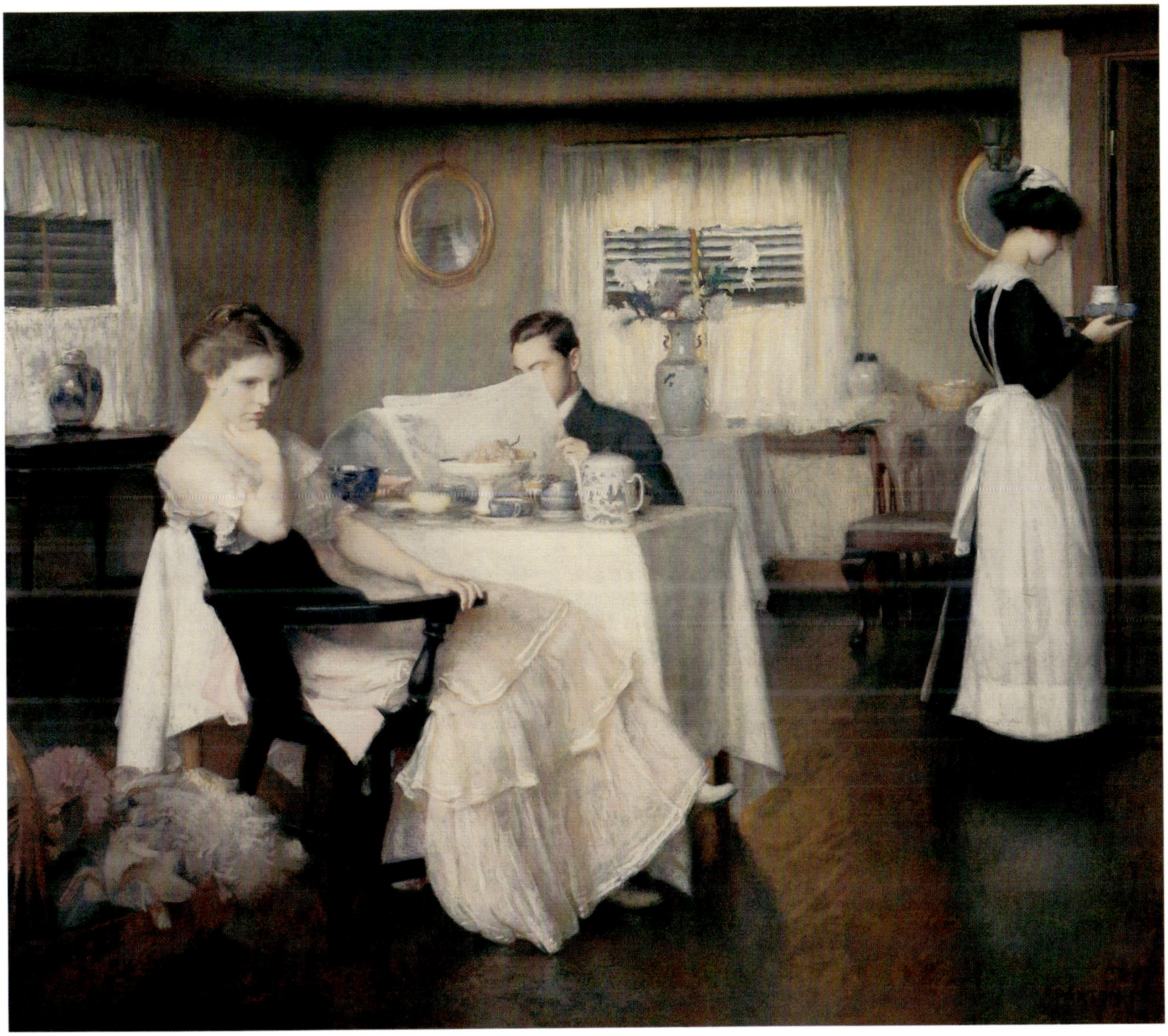

Marguerite Stuber Pearson (1898-1978)

Marguerite Pearson's life was one of courageous commitment to her art in the face of an enormous physical handicap and frequent ill-health. Until her death in 1978 she carried on the tradition of Boston School painting as she had learned it under Edmund C. Tarbell. She painted interiors with figures in a manner that is an amalgam of the styles of William Paxton and Tarbell, but she also devoted considerable time to still-life painting. In these works her approach recalls that of Emil Carlsen, but her colors are stronger, and their texture is more painterly.

This work is not dated, but since Pearson exhibited a painting that was very similar in 1929, it must date from about the same time. That work, titled *Old Brass*, features a nearly identical glass bottle, and the same brass tray with fruit, rumpled tablecloth, and table that appear here. It was shown at the Seventh Annual Exhibition of the North Shore Arts Association of Gloucester and was mentioned in an important review: "from Marguerite S. Pearson, a new exhibitor, came a superbly painted still life, 'Old Brass' " ("Notes: A Notable Exhibition in Gloucester," *American Magazine of Art* 20 [October 1929], p. 587, ill. p. 580).

This work was acquired by Dr. and Mrs. McDonough directly from the artist, long a personal friend.

Ex coll.:
The artist, Rockport, Massachusetts, until 1978; Dr. and Mrs. John J. McDonough, Youngstown, Ohio.

Still Life with Brass
c. 1925-30

oil on canvas
30 x 36 in. (76.2 x 91.4 cm.)
Signed, lower left: Marguerite S. Pearson

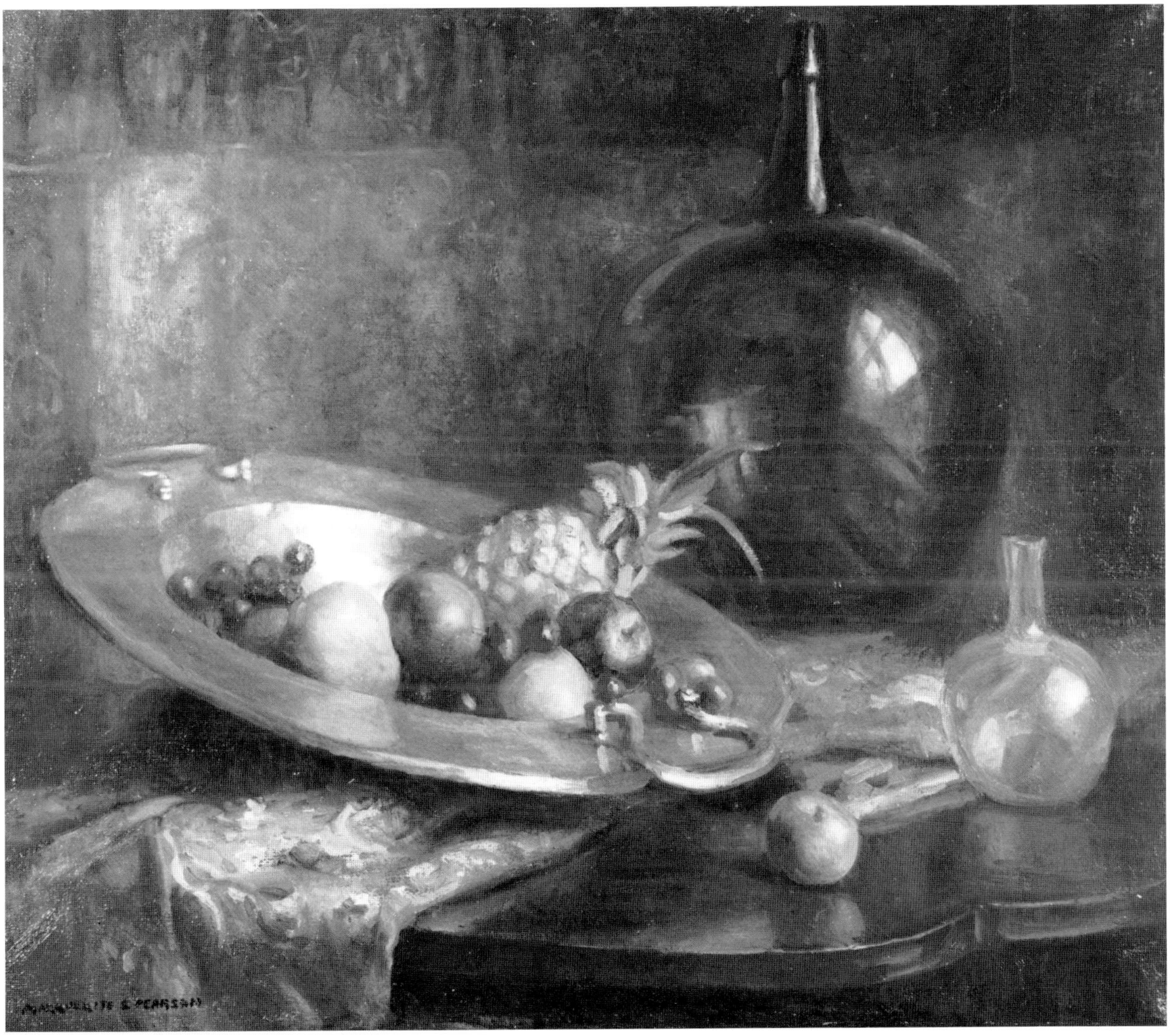

Edward Henry Potthast (1857-1927)

An extremely shy and retiring man, Potthast gave out little information about himself, his travels, or his working methods. It appears, however, that he moved about in search of subject matter quite a bit and that he sketched outdoors a great deal, subsequently working up his sketches into larger pictures in his studio. His forte was the representation of beach scenes featuring children and adults at play or simply relaxing in the sunshine. These he painted again and again from about 1903 until the end of his life. As might be expected, he was accused of being monotonous, but, as a contemporary noted in a brochure published by the Macbeth Gallery, "When a man paints a theme as well as Potthast paints seashore subjects, we forgive him for sticking to it to the exclusion of other subjects" (quoted in essay by Arlene Jacobowitz in Chapellier Galleries, 1969, unpaged).

Potthast seldom dated his beach scenes and only infrequently identified their locations in their titles. It is, however, possible to draw inferences from comparisons made with known, dated subjects. In the case of *Hourtide*, its date seems to be about 1920 and its location Manhattan Beach. A work by that title illustrated in a Macbeth Gallery brochure in 1921 exhibits numerous correspondences with this one. Among them are the high line of the water, an umbrella positioned at the corner of the canvas, the figure of a woman seen from the back and looking down, and a number of figures visible only from the waist up in the middle ground (Macbeth Gallery, New York, 1921, *Exhibition of Intimate Paintings*, no. 54, *Manhattan Beach*; see also no. 55, *A July Day*). In addition, the active brushwork and the patch-like areas of color in *Hourtide* conform better to Potthast's late style when the influence of the works of Maurice Prendergast became more obvious.

That Potthast carefully arranged the composition of his seemingly spontaneous beach scenes can scarcely be doubted. In this work the two standing figures in the middle ground were added as an afterthought in order to improve it.

References:
Chapellier Galleries, Inc., New York, *Edward Henry Potthast, 1857-1927* (1968), essay by Arlene Jacobowitz, no. 7, ill. in color on cover.

Ex coll.:
Chapellier Galleries, Inc., New York, 1968; Joan Patterson Roberts, New Canaan, Connecticut; sale, Sotheby Parke-Bernet, Inc., New York, April 21, 1978, no. 95; Dr. and Mrs. John J. McDonough, Youngstown, Ohio.

Hourtide
c. 1920

oil on canvas
24 x 30 in. (61 x 76.2 cm.)
Signed, lower left: E. Potthast

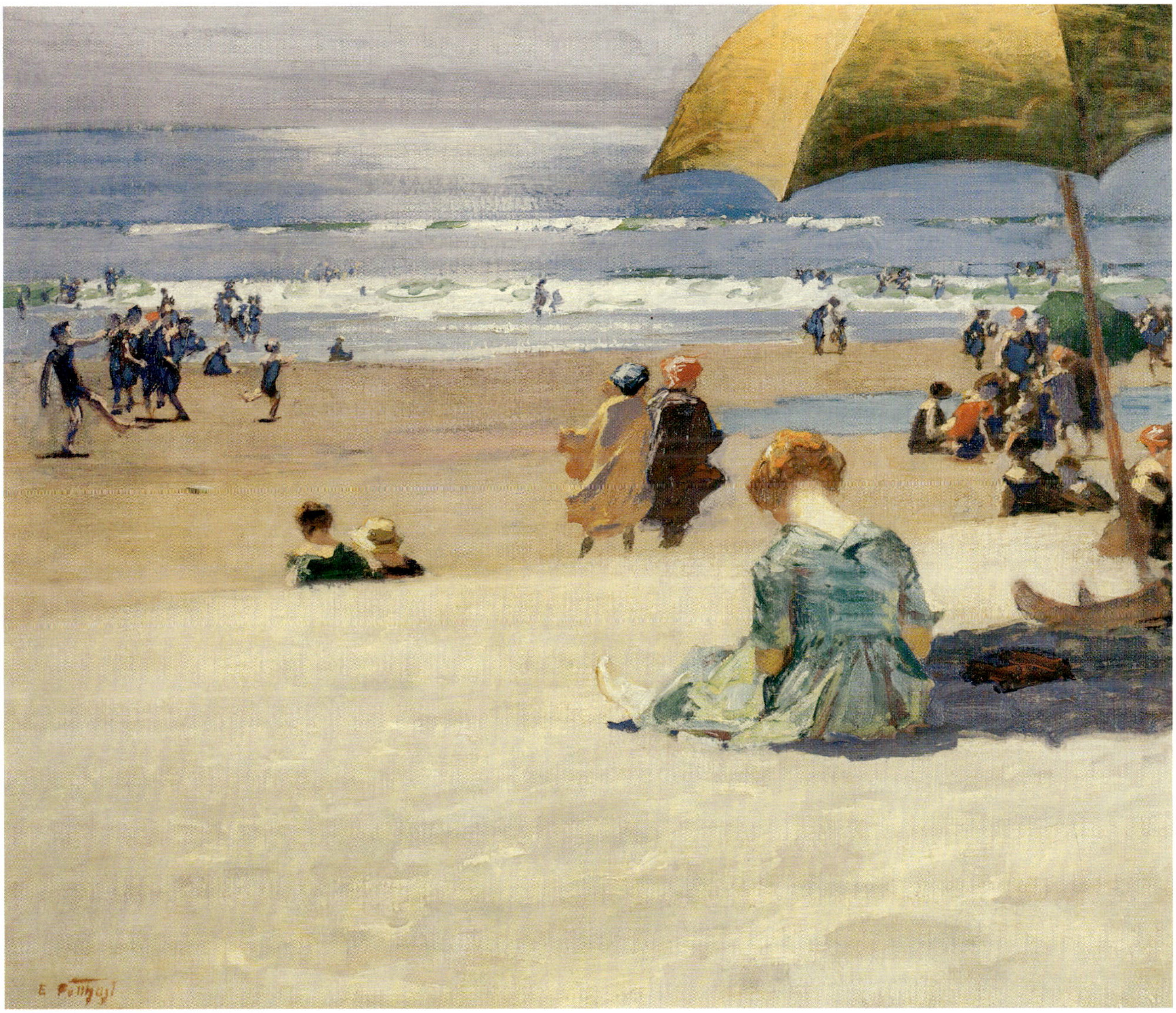

Maurice Brazil Prendergast
(1859-1924)

The content and chronology of Prendergast's style have always presented extremely difficult problems to students of his work. Most of his oils and watercolors are undated, as is this example, and possess titles which do not disclose their subject matter. Comparison with other, better documented works by the artist sometimes leads to the resolution of questions, but frequently also to further confusion. Prendergast, it seems, cared little for such matters and was only concerned with presenting the viewer with an arrangement of color.

In the case of *New England Beach Scene*, a firm association can be made on stylistic grounds with the watercolor known as *Marblehead Rocks*, which Prendergast sent to the landmark Armory Show of 1913 (private collection, ill. in University of Maryland Art Gallery, College Park, Maryland, 1976, *Maurice Prendergast*, no. 42, p. 108). If this establishes the location of *New England Beach Scene*, however, it does not disclose its date of execution: *Marblehead Rocks* may have been finished in 1912 or as early as 1897-98. To further confuse matters, *New England Beach Scene*, while in the possession of Mrs. Malcolm McBride, was published once as painted in 1907-08 (W.M. Milliken, 1926) and once as done in 1896 (Whitney Museum of American Art, 1934). A likely explanation for this discrepancy is the work itself, which, while being closely linked in subject matter to the beach scenes Prendergast painted in the late 1890s, is far more freely executed than those works. Is it possible that Prendergast would have sent to the Armory Show a work he had executed fourteen or fifteen years previously, or are both *Marblehead Rocks* and *New England Beach Scene* of later date? In the absence of further evidence the question is unanswerable. What is certain is that both of these works are steps in the direction of Prendergast's later style, when he changed, as Royal Cortissoz put it, "from a fairly close and clear definition of objects to the enwrapping of them in a broad investiture of color" (*The Herald Tribune* [New York], February 25, 1934).

References:
William Matthewson Milliken, "Maurice Prendergast, American Artist," *The Arts* 9 (April 1926), p. 189, ill. as *New England Beach* in the possession of Mrs. Malcolm L. McBride, Cleveland, Ohio, and dated 1907-08.

Exhibited:
Cleveland Museum of Art, 1926, *Maurice Prendergast Memorial Exhibition*, unpublished checklist of watercolors, no. 22, lent by Kraushaar Galleries, New York; Whitney Museum of American Art, New York, 1934, *Maurice Prendergast Memorial Exhibition*, no. 24, as *New England Beach* in the collection of Mrs. Malcolm L. McBride, dated 1896.

Ex coll.:
Kraushaar Galleries, Inc., New York, until 1926; Mrs. Malcolm L. McBride, Cleveland Ohio, 1926-about 1960; Kraushaar Galleries, Inc., New York; Joan Patterson Roberts, New Canaan, Connecticut, about 1960; sale, Sotheby Parke-Bernet, Inc., New York, April 21, 1978, no. 84; Dr. and Mrs. John J. McDonough, Youngstown, Ohio.

New England Beach Scene
c. 1896-1912

watercolor on paper
13¾ x 19¾ in. (34.9 x 50.2 cm.)
Signed, lower left: Prendergast

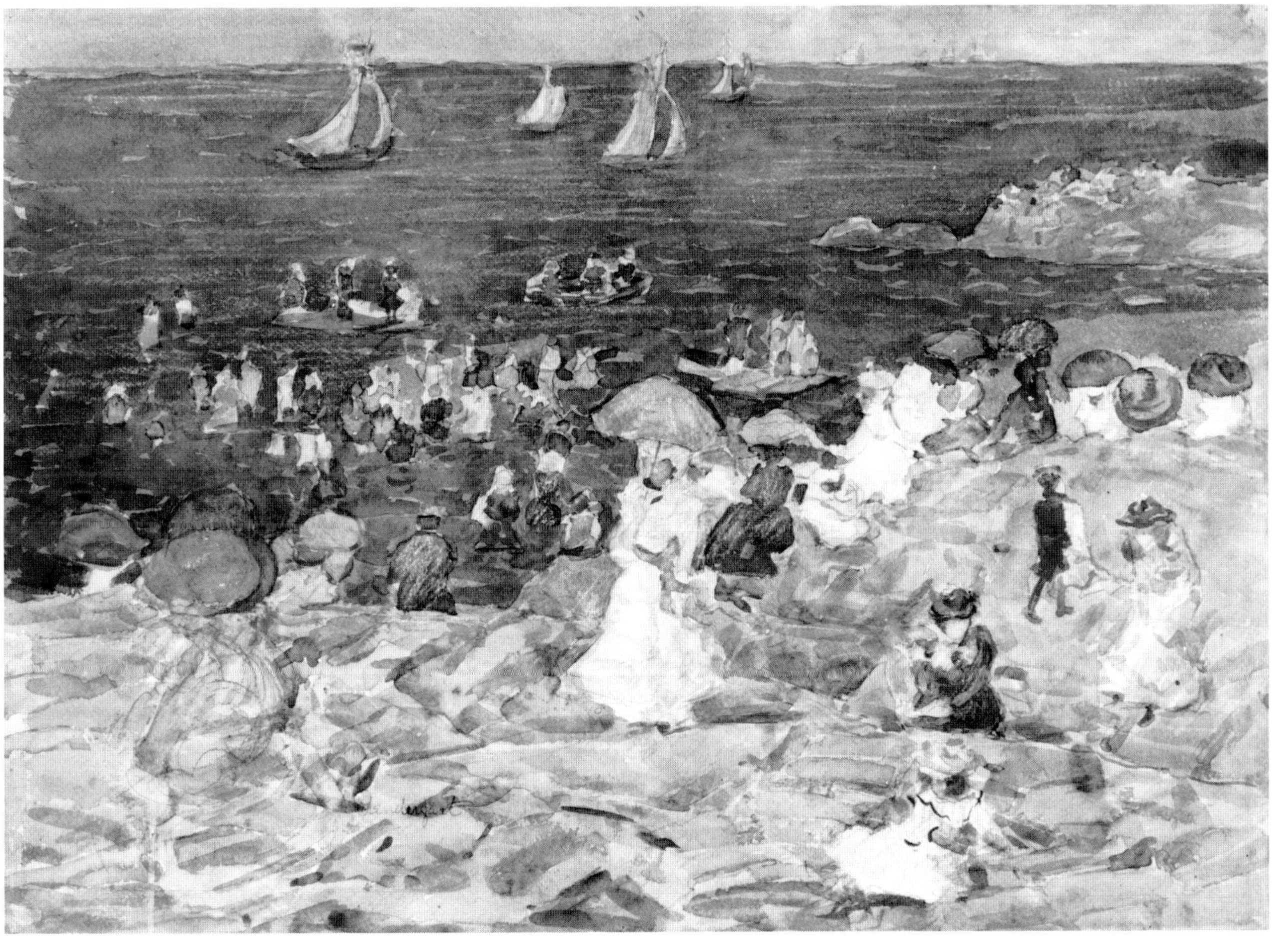

Edward Willis Redfield (1869-1965)

The subtle coloring and juicy execution of this work are typical of Redfield's mature style. Although the scene represented has not been identified in documents, it is possible to conclude from comparisons with other Redfield landscapes that it is in the vicinity of Center Bridge, Pennsylvania. Redfield had bought property there in 1898 and after about 1910 devoted himself to depicting snow scenes in the vicinity. The Delaware River and the hills of New Jersey were often in the background of these scenes, as indeed they are in this work.

To the end of his life Redfield remained a painter committed to realistic representation and to an Impressionist-influenced technique. However, it is clear from this work that his spontaneous and energetic style, with equal attention paid to every area of the canvas, had something in common with the all-over principles of composition and spontaneous execution espoused by American abstract artists of the post-World War II generation. Redfield painted his pictures outdoors "at one go," as he put it, often spending long, uninterrupted hours in the cold. The result was an immediacy in his paintings that was quite unlike the tamer Impressionism of the 1880s and 90s and gained him a number of followers, among them Walter Elmer Schofield and George Gardner Symons. They were frequently referred to as the Pennsylvania School or the Bucks County School, though Schofield and Symons seldom worked in Pennsylvania.

References:
"The 6th Annual Exhibition of Selected Paintings by American Artists," *Academy Notes* 6 (July 1911), p. 93, commenting on the works then on view at the Buffalo Fine Arts Academy notes: "Edward W. Redfield has produced a masterpiece in the superb work called 'The Grey Veil,' which holds one of the places of honor in this exhibition. It also had a most important hanging in the recent exhibition at the Pennsylvania Academy of the Fine Arts. This picture should never be allowed to leave Buffalo. It is one of Mr. Redfield's most important works, and has all his strength of technique, with an exquisite refinement. It is a masterpiece"; Thomas Folk, "Edward Redfield: Pennsylvania Impressionist," *Art and Antiques* 4 (March-April 1981), p. 63, ill. in color but misdated c. 1925-40.

Exhibited:
Pennsylvania Academy of the Fine Arts, Philadelphia, 1911, *106th Annual Exhibition*, no. 311; Albright Art Gallery, Buffalo Fine Arts Academy, Buffalo, New York, 1911, *6th Annual Exhibition of Selected Paintings by American Artists*, no. 106, ill. p. 62.

Ex coll.:
Family of the artist, Doylestown, Pennsylvania, until 1979; Vose Galleries, Inc., Boston, until 1980; Dr. and Mrs. John J. McDonough, Youngstown, Ohio.

The Grey Veil
c. 1910

oil on canvas
38 x 50 in. (96.5 x 127 cm.)
Signed, lower left: E.W. Redfield

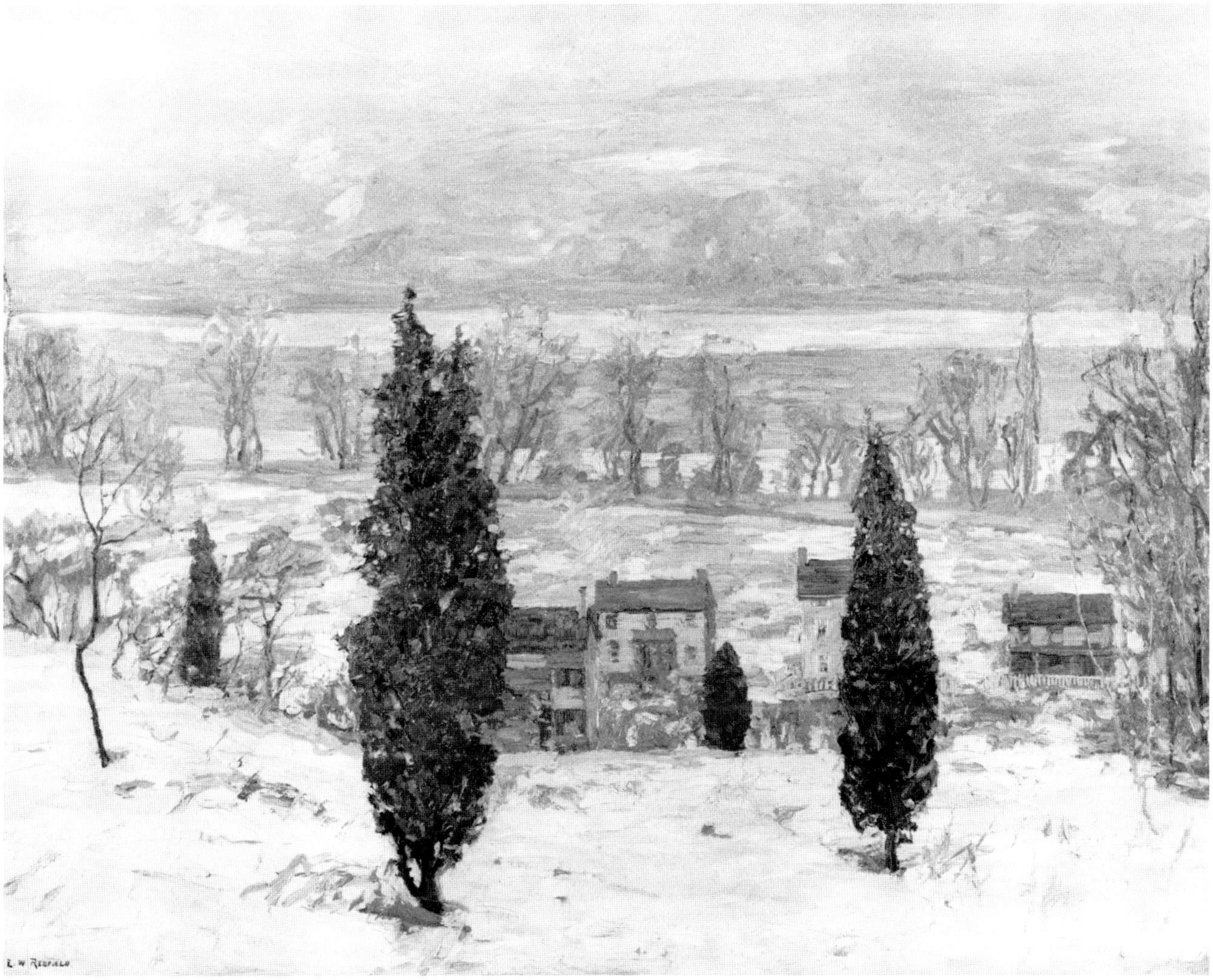

Robert Reid
(1862-1929)

Not a great deal of attention has been paid to Robert Reid's easel paintings of the 1890s. During most of this time he was occupied as a mural painter working on the decoration of the Manufactures and Liberal Arts Building at the Chicago World's Columbian Exposition (1892), of the Library of Congress (1897), and of the Appellate Courthouse in New York (1899). In between commissions and during vacations, however, he continued to produce works on canvas that he frequently exhibited. Of these, the best known paintings are of single figures of women in an outdoor setting surrounded by flowers or foliage. Less well known are the landscapes, which are infrequent in his work.

When purchased by Dr. and Mrs. McDonough at auction this painting was called *Forest Brook*. It is likely, however, that it is the work titled *The Brook* which Reid exhibited at Durand-Ruel's in New York and at Carnegie Institute, Pittsburgh, in 1899. The style in which it is painted certainly corresponds to Reid's work about this time. It consists of long, broad strokes on a coarse canvas with two or three colors dragged in each stroke. Of Reid's paintings, Christian Brinton further noted: "Technically, his work while free and sometimes even careless, displays numerous welcome qualities. The stroke is broad and virile, the surfaces agreeably broken, and the various tones subtly modulated" (Christian Brinton, "Robert Reid, Decorative Impressionist," *Arts & Decoration* 2 [November 1911], p. 15).

Exhibited:
Durand-Ruel Galleries, Inc., New York, 1899, *Ten American Painters*, unnumbered checklist, listed as *The Brook*; Carnegie Institute, Pittsburgh, 1899, *Fourth Annual Exhibition*, no. 192, as *The Brook*.

Ex coll.:
Mrs. William Henry Bliss; Mr. and Mrs. Robert Woods Bliss, Washington, D.C.; Dumbarton Oaks Collection, Harvard University, Washington, D.C.; sale, Sotheby Parke-Bernet, Inc., New York, December 12, 1975, no. 82; Mr. and Mrs. John W. Graves, Wichita, Kansas; sale, Sotheby Parke-Bernet, Inc., New York, April 21, 1978, no. 75; Dr. and Mrs. John J. McDonough, Youngstown, Ohio.

The Brook
c. 1899

oil on canvas
26½ x 30½ in. (67.3 x 77.5 cm.)
Signed, lower left: Robert Reid

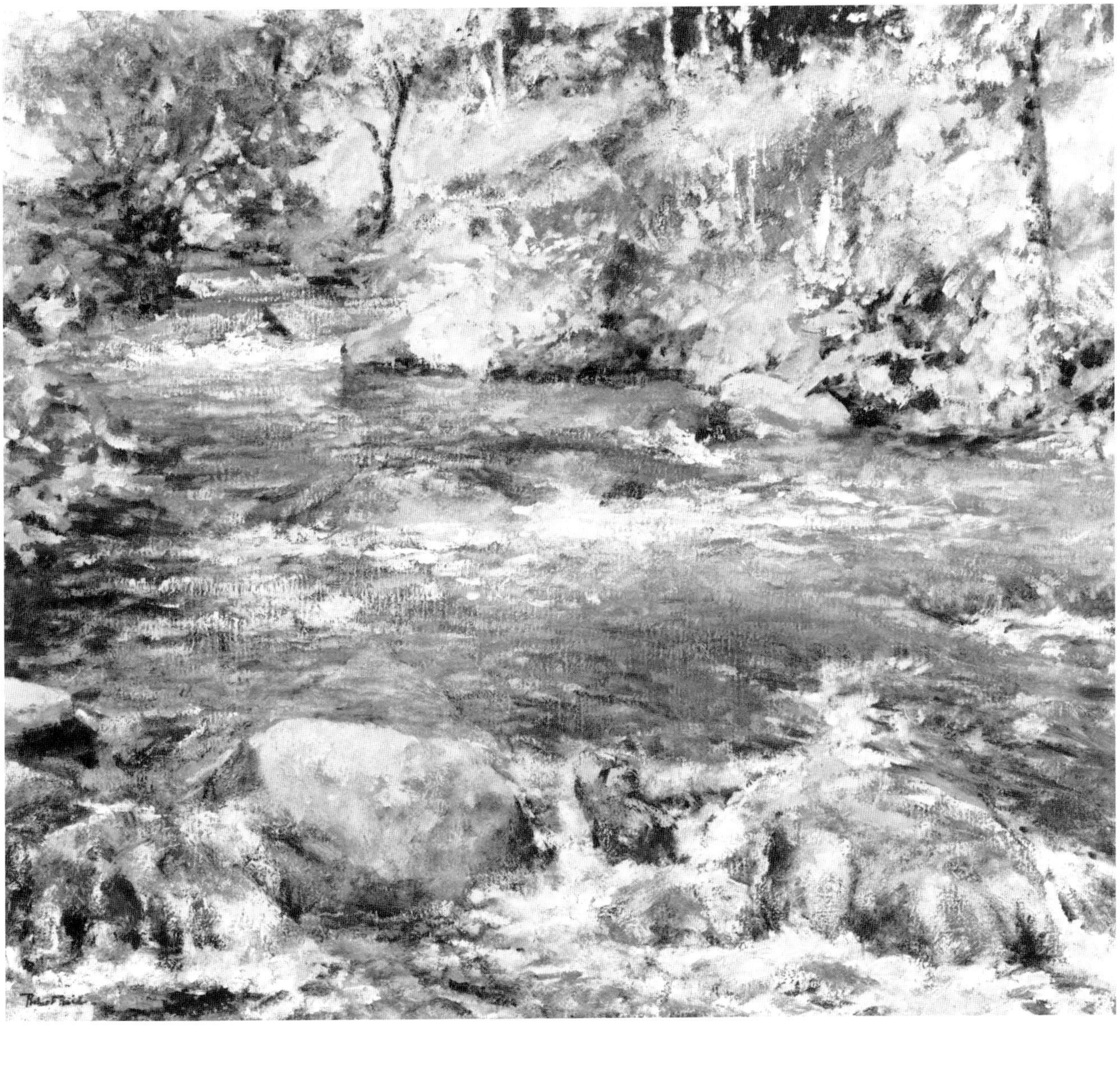

Louis Ritman
(1889-1963)

Sometime around 1912 the Chicago-born Louis Ritman, a recent convert to Impressionism, rented a house in Giverny. He was only about twenty-two years old, but he had already exhibited great promise and had sent two works to the Paris Salon in 1910. In Giverny he probably met Monet as well as the Americans Theodore Earl Butler and Frederick Frieseke who had also settled there. Until 1915, when he returned to Chicago, Ritman lived at Giverny painting in a style that is somewhat reminiscent of Monet's, though his brushwork is broader and much less dense than the master's. Some of his finest Impressionist works were painted at this time. Later in his career, his style changed a good deal and conformed more to the type of Realism prevalent in this country in the 20s and 30s.

Although this painting has been identified by its present title for some time, an old label attached to the back calls it *Garden in Giverny*, thus establishing where it was painted and corroborating the date in the signature. The abundant presence of hollyhocks further associates it with another work of this period, *Hollyhocks*, purchased in 1915 by the city of Chicago for its permanent collection.

Many of Ritman's works executed from 1912 to 1914 were exhibited at the Art Institute of Chicago in February of 1915. At the time, one critic noted: "His figure paintings are more individual and more generally discussed than his spotty sunlit flower gardens, which, while clever, are similar in style to the works of some of his contemporaries" (E. M. Stuart, quoted in Richard H. Love, *The Paintings of Louis Ritman (1889-1963)* [1975], p. 6). The critic probably had in mind the works of Frederick Frieseke with whom Ritman was unjustly grouped as a follower for most of his early career.

References:
Campanile Galleries, Inc., Chicago, *American Paintings* (1977), p. 8, ill. in color, erroneously states it is dated 1909.

Ex coll.:
Private collection, Paris, until 1977; Campanile Galleries, Inc., Chicago, 1977-78; Dr. and Mrs. John J. McDonough, Youngstown, Ohio.

Lady in Garden with Hollyhocks
1914

oil on canvas
32 x 26 in. (81.3 x 66 cm.)
Signed and dated, lower right: L. Ritman 1914

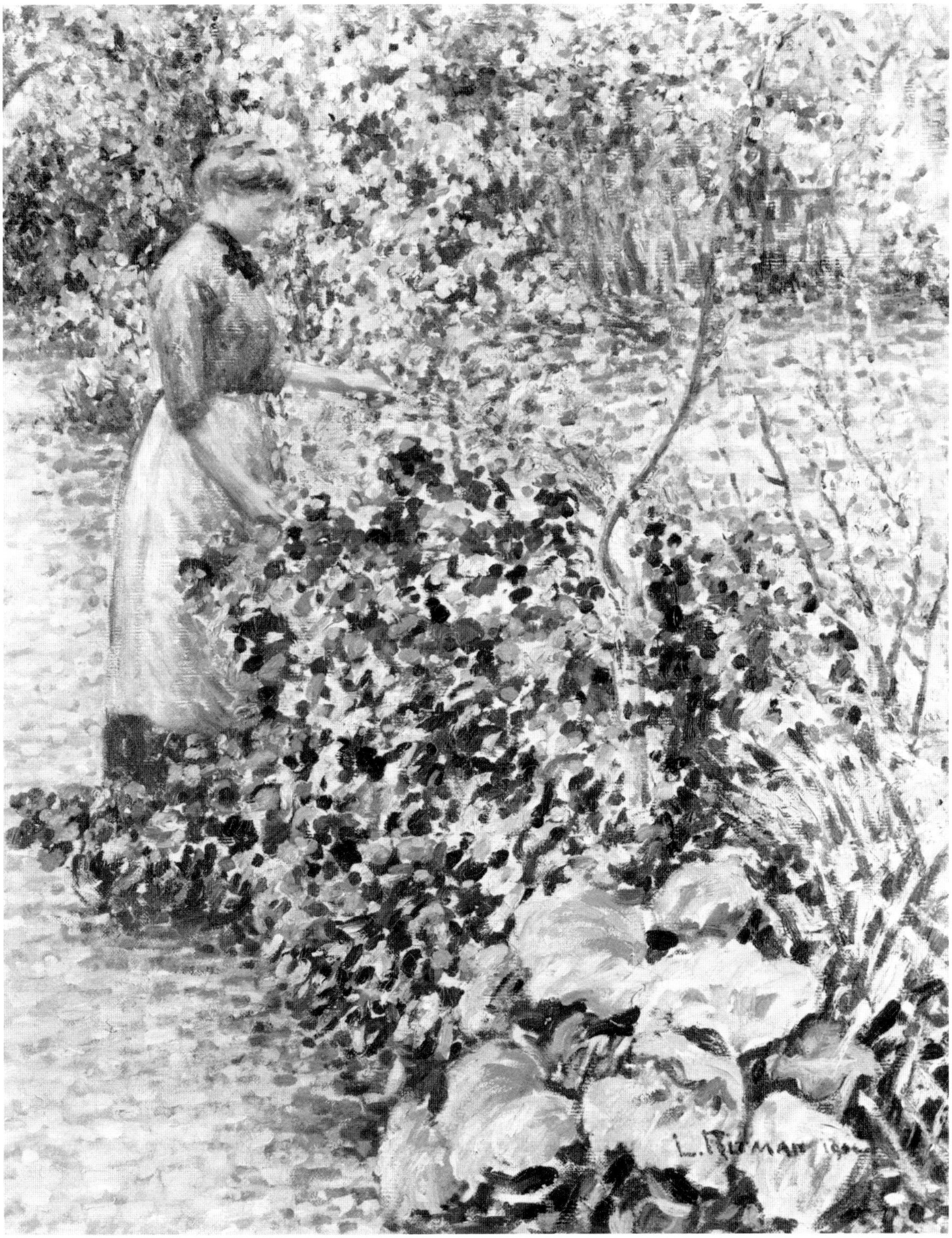

Theodore Robinson
(1852-1896)

Although Robinson was one of the few American artists working in Giverny who was actually befriended by Claude Monet, his Impressionist style did not develop along the lines of Monet's. Whereas the French artist analyzed what he saw in strokes and colors that are essentially independent of the forms they combine to represent, Robinson, like many other American Impressionists, was more concerned with the clear definition of outlines and objects. His colors are not usually juxtaposed so as to produce another color when viewed at a distance, and his figures almost always reveal the modeling of traditional academic technique. Frequently, as was the case in this work, he relied on photographs to guide him in composition and in figural representation.

Three versions of *The Layette* are known (Baur, 1946, nos. 129, 130, and 131). The largest one, now at the Corcoran Gallery of Art, Washington, D.C., was painted in 1892. On October 30 of that year Robinson noted in his diary: "Worked a.m. in Gill's Garden with Yvonne on large Layette," indicating that he must have also used a model as well as photographs in executing some of his works (quoted in Baltimore Museum of Art, 1973, *Theodore Robinson, 1852-1896*, exhibition catalogue by Sona Johnston, p. 49). Because the diary firmly dates this version, and because the smaller ones are thought to precede it, these have been dated about 1891 or 1892. Further chronological accuracy is impossible, but it would appear from a comparison with the photograph Robinson used (collection of Ira Spanierman, New York) that the McDonough painting is the earliest in the series. The position of the girl's hands as well as of the tree and its branches faithfully follows the photographic image, whereas, in the other two versions, it has been changed.

This work was painted at Giverny, where Robinson returned after a brief trip to New York in 1888-89. It was at this time that his mature style developed, and he came to identify with the goals of Impressionism.

References:
John I.H. Baur, *Theodore Robinson, 1852-1896* (1946), p. 67, no. 129, lists it and quotes Robinson's diary, August 10, 1892: "Mr. Marquand bought my little 'Layette' for $300. for his partner Mr. Blake of Boston"; Eliot Clark, *Theodore Robinson: His Life and Art* (1979), p. 52, pl. 1.

Exhibited:
Danforth Museum, Framingham, Massachusetts, 1978, *American Impressionist Painting*, no cat.

Ex coll.:
Arthur W. Blake, Brookline, Massachusetts; Mrs. Beatrice Blake Nickerson; Henry G. Nickerson, Dedham, Massachusetts; sale, Sotheby Parke-Bernet, Inc., New York, October 27, 1977, no. 45; Steven Straw Company, Inc., Newburyport, Massachusetts, 1977-78; Dr. and Mrs. John J. McDonough, Youngstown, Ohio.

The Layette
1891 or 1892

oil on canvas
23 x 15 in. (58.4 x 38.1 cm.)
Signed, lower right: Th. Robinson

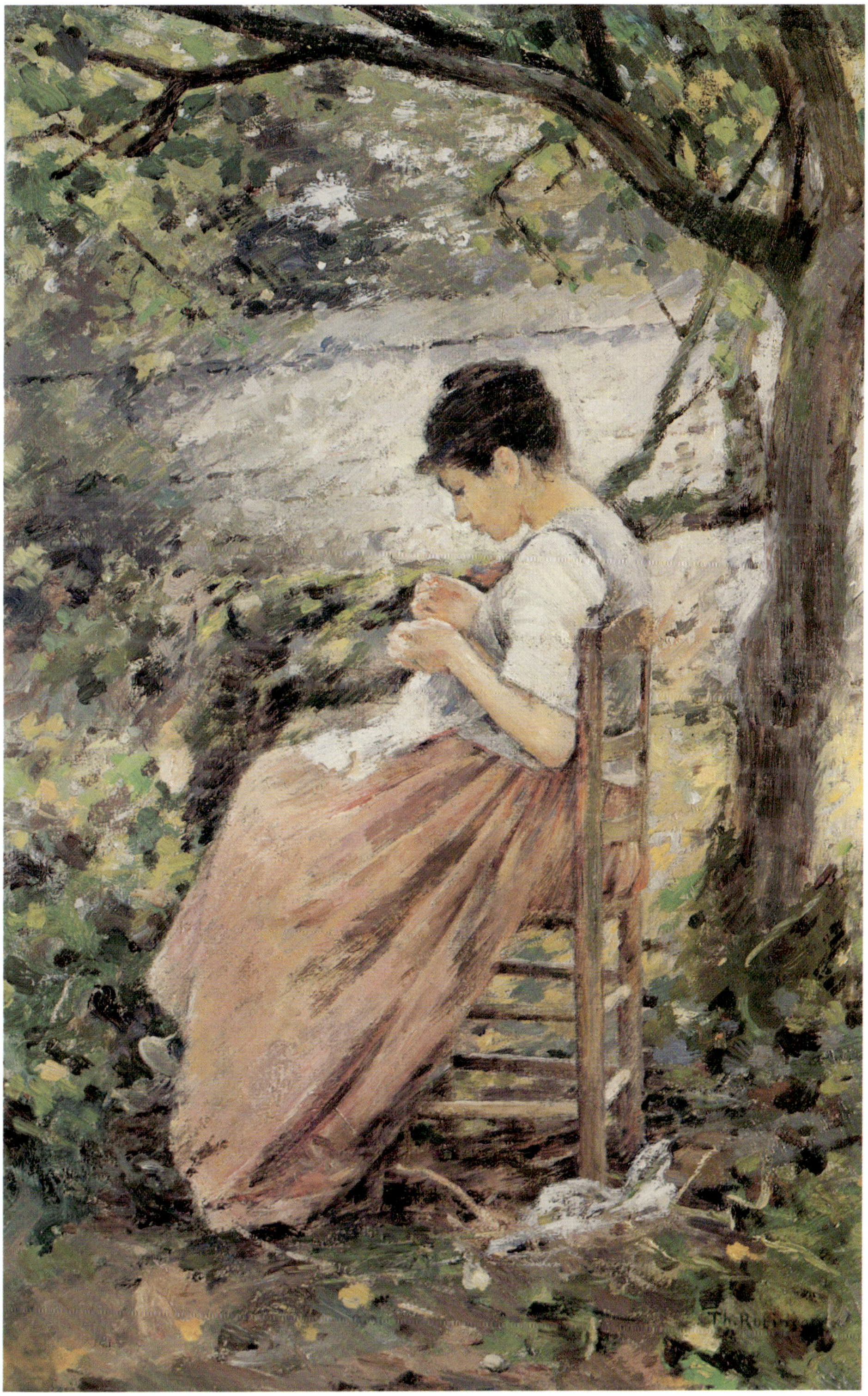

Walter Russell
(1871-1963)

This work was thought to have been painted by Russell in 1923 based on a possible reading of the date in the lower right corner of the painting. However, judging from the turn-of-the-century costumes of the women and children depicted, a far more likely date would probably be 1898. At this time Russell was art editor for *Collier's* weekly and was much involved in writing children's stories, an activity he had long given up by 1923.

No connection has been found between this highly accomplished work and the stories by Russell examined by the author, but it seems likely in view of the number of children represented, and of their visually dominant position in the painting, that it is related to or derived from one of these works of fiction.

Ex coll.:
Sale, Sotheby Parke-Bernet, Inc. (PB 84), New York, June 4 and 5, 1980, no. 255; Dr. and Mrs. John J. McDonough, Youngstown, Ohio.

At the Seashore
probably 1898

oil on canvas
28¼ x 36 in. (71.8 x 91.4 cm.)
Signed and dated, lower right: W. Russell 98 (indistinctly)

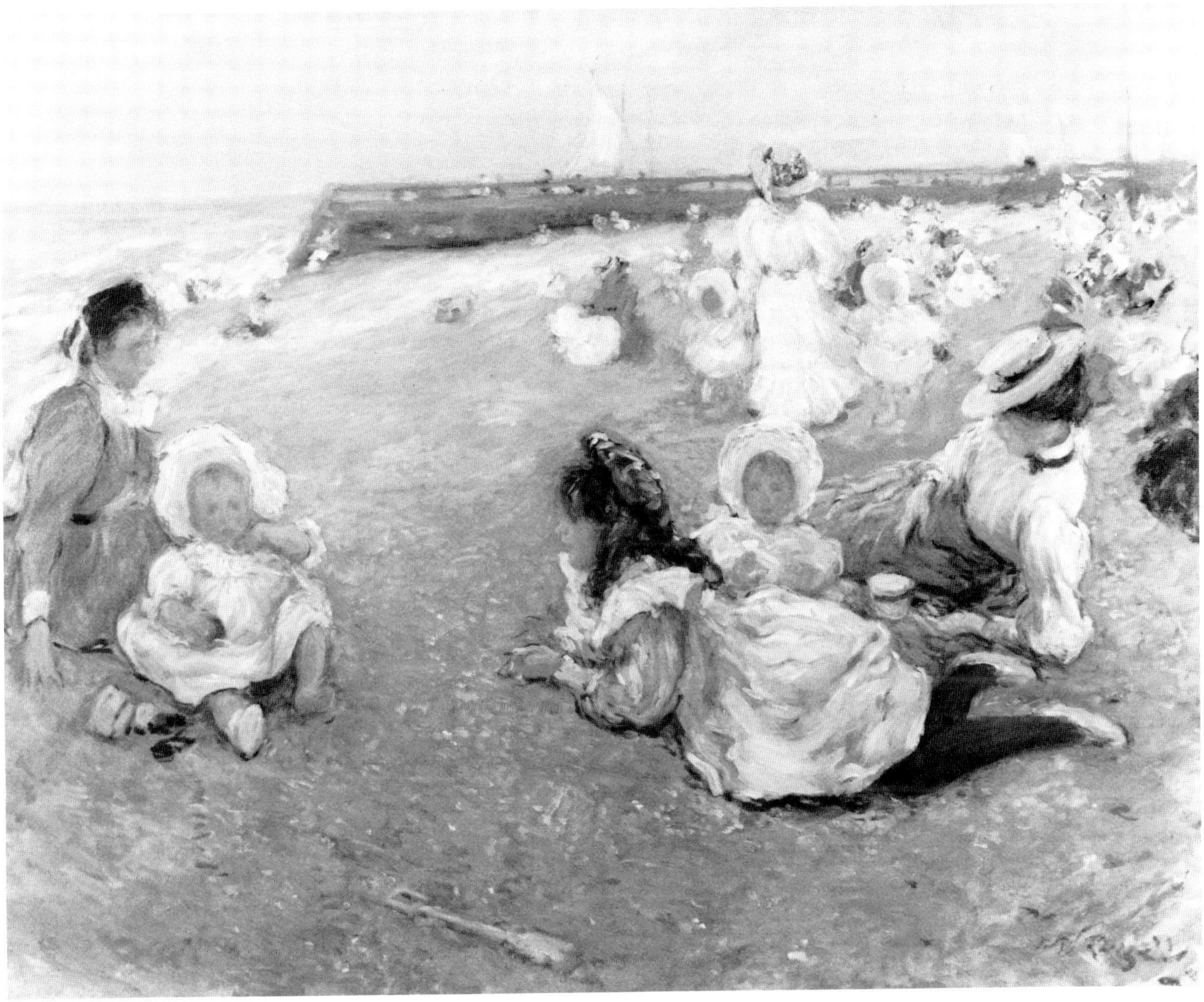

John Singer Sargent (1856-1925)

In 1885 Sargent began spending his summers at the remote Cotswold village of Broadway, a retreat for young English and American artists and writers. In this sympathetic milieu, he acquired several close friends, including Edmund Gosse, a distinguished poet, author, and critic. Sargent painted this portrait of Gosse's daughter on the occasion of her eighth birthday, September 14, 1885. Teresa Gosse has noted that the painting was created upon her return from a picnic with bunches of autumn colchicum. Pleased with Teresa's red hair, wreath of mauve flowers, and white dress, Sargent quickly painted a sketch of her on a canvas already covered with a landscape scene (Leeds Art Galleries, 1979, p. 40). The bold, fluent brushwork and high-keyed, luminous palette reveal Sargent's growing interest in Impressionism.

Edmund Gosse described Sargent's experimental aim in Broadway as "to acquire the habit of reproducing precisely whatever met his vision without the slightest previous 'arrangement' of detail, the painter's business being, not to pick and choose, but to render the effect before him, whatever it may be" (Evan Charteris, *John Sargent* [1927, reprint 1972], p. 77). Sargent made several similarly vivid studies of children at this time, including his Broadway masterpiece, *Carnation, Lily, Lily, Rose*, 1885-86 (Tate Gallery, London). He also painted two portraits of Edmund Gosse in 1886 (Brotherton Library, Leeds; National Portrait Gallery, London).

G. S.

References:
David McKibbin, *Sargent's Boston* (1956), p. 98; Charles Merrill Mount, *John Singer Sargent* (1969), p. 440, no. 8512.

Exhibited:
Graves Art Gallery, Sheffield, 1954, *Paintings by Edwardian Artists*, no. 34: City Museum and Art Gallery, Birmingham, 1964, *Exhibition of Works by John Singer Sargent*, no. 12; Leeds Art Galleries; National Portrait Gallery, London; and Detroit Institute of Arts, 1979, *John Singer Sargent and the Edwardian Age*, catalogue by James Lomax and Richard Ormond, no. 22, p. 40.

Ex coll.:
Mrs. Edmund Gosse; Sylvia Gosse; Miss Jennifer Gosse; sale, Sotheby Parke-Bernet, Inc., London, March 8, 1978, no. 66; Steven Straw Company, Inc., Newburyport, Massachusetts, 1978; Dr. and Mrs. John J. McDonough, Youngstown, Ohio.

Teresa Gosse
1885

oil on canvas
24 x 20 in. (61 x 50.8 cm.)
Signed and inscribed upper left: To Mrs. Gosse John S. Sargent

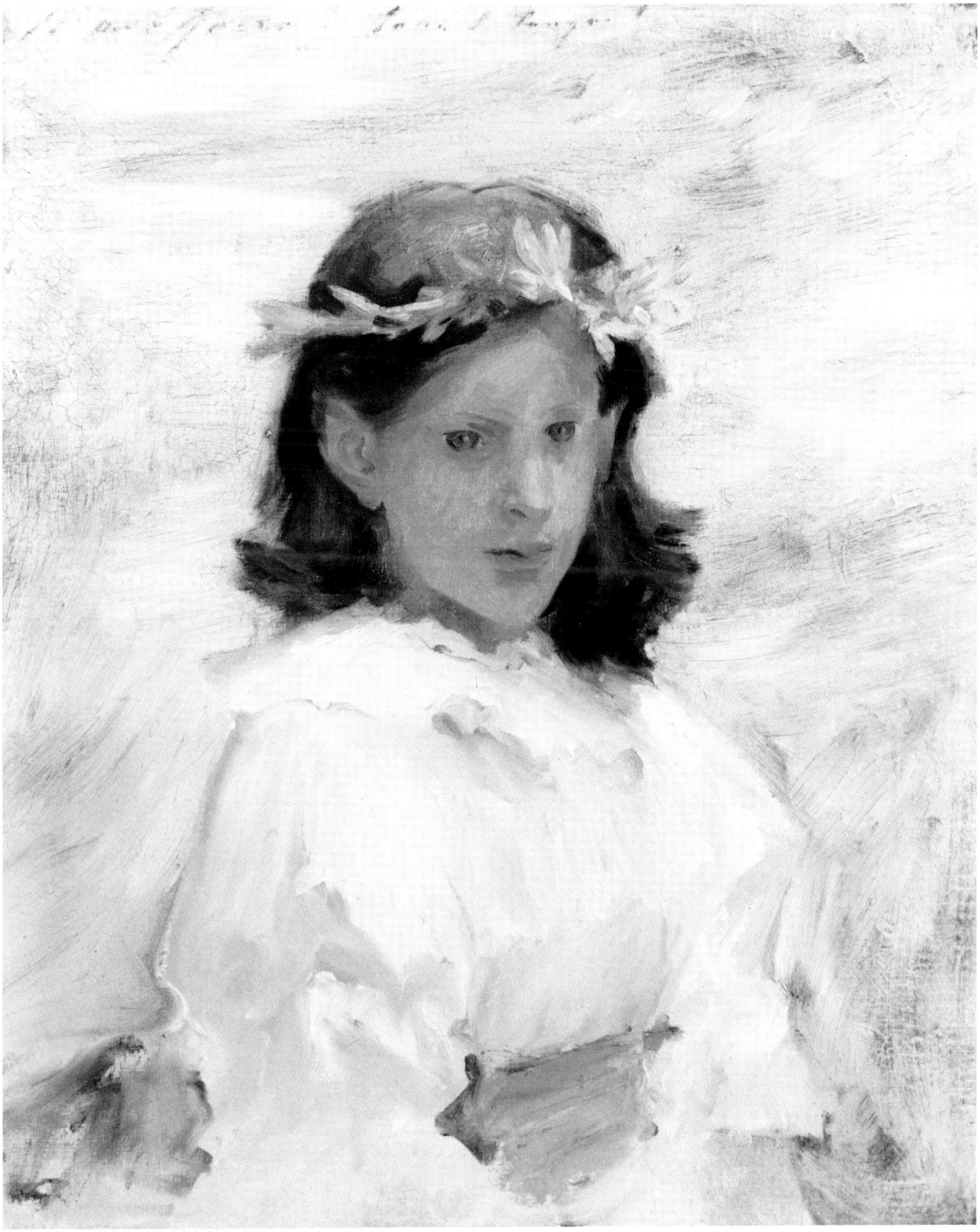

John Singer Sargent
(1856-1925)

The small size and bold, loose brushwork of this painting suggest that it is an informal portrait sketch. Unlike his practice in formal portraiture, Sargent here has freely defined the body and dress of the figure in terms of flat, tonal areas of color. The broadly painted curtain backdrop and dramatic, artificial lighting suggest a stage setting. Sargent painted portraits of the actresses Ellen Terry, Eleonora Duse, and Ada Rehan in 1889, about 1893, and 1894, respectively (Tate Gallery, London; collection of Mr. and Mrs. Paul Amir; Metropolitan Museum of Art, New York). Miss Rehan is depicted in front of a similarly fluid rendition of a theatrical backdrop. Although the McDonough sketch does not appear to be directly related to these paintings, it may well be a contemporary portrait sketch of an actress or someone connected with the theater.

Even though this work is not a plein-air sketch, the immediacy and verve of its brushwork are an outgrowth of Sargent's impressionist studies at Broadway, Fladbury, and Giverny in the late 1880s.

G. S.

Ex coll.:
Family of the artist; his niece, Mrs. Hugo Pittman; sale, Adam A. Weschler and Son, Inc., Washington, D.C., December 7, 8, and 9, 1979, no. 1118; Dr. and Mrs. John J. McDonough, Youngstown, Ohio.

A Lady in Evening Gown
probably c. 1890-95

oil on canvas
17 x 15 in. (43.2 x 38.1 cm.)
Signed, lower right: John S. Sargent

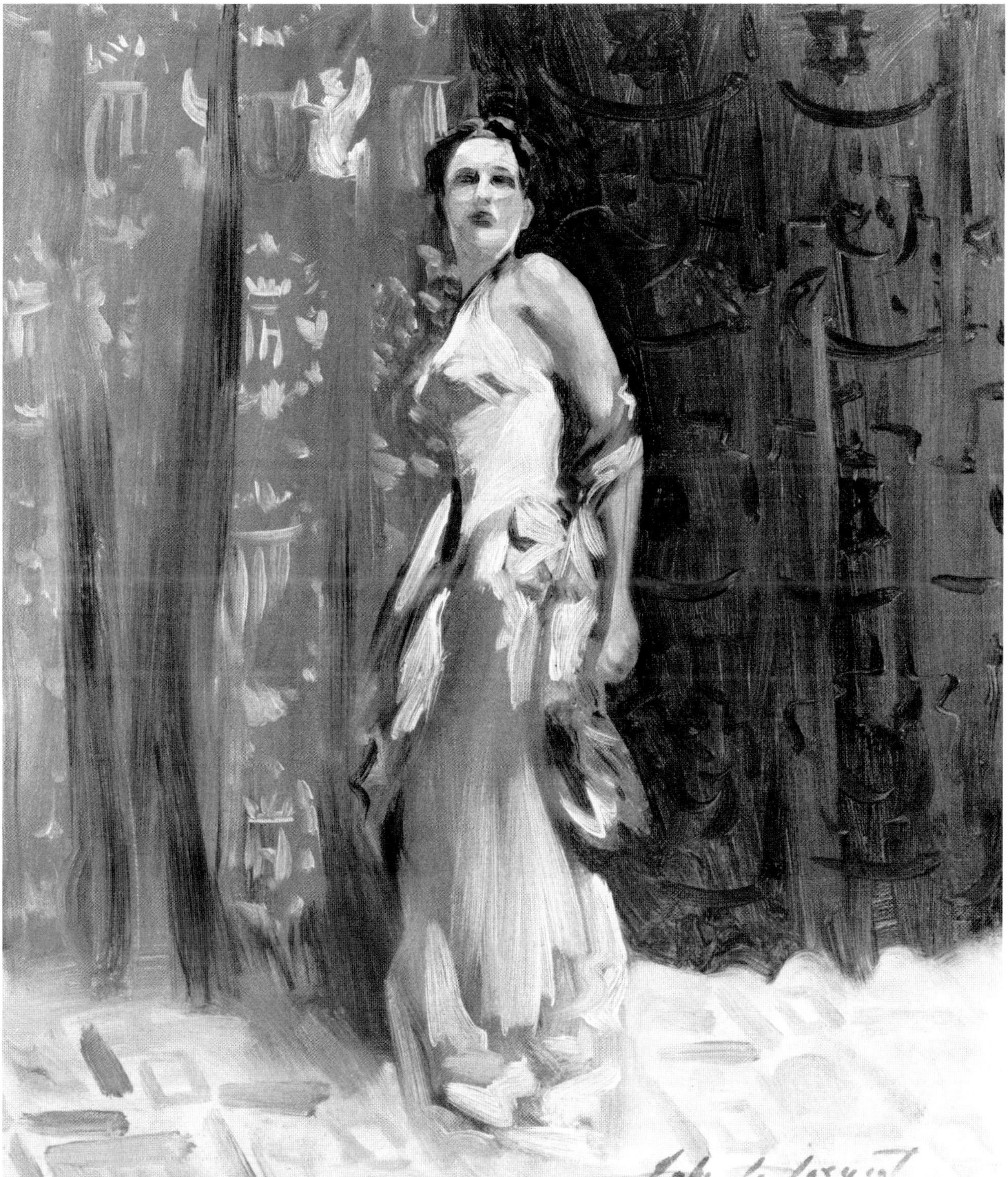

Walter Elmer Schofield
(1867-1944)

This work is part of a series of pictures of cottages in Cornwall and Devonshire which Schofield completed and exhibited between about 1920 and 1927. The specific location of McLegrenow Farm is not known, but it was definitely in Cornwall and very likely in the vicinity of Truro. Another work by Schofield, *Harmony Cot* (unlocated, exhibited at Macbeth Gallery, New York, 1922, *Thirty Paintings by Thirty Artists*, no. 23, ill.), bears numerous similarities with *McLegrenow Farm* and is known to represent the birthplace near Truro of the British painter John Opie.

With its strong diagonals and clearly defined space, *McLegrenow Farm* well illustrates the compositional clarity for which Schofield's works were admired. This almost academic approach combined with a vigorous and colorful execution that was clearly influenced by, but did not adhere to, Monet's analytical practice, was something Schofield shared with Edward Redfield, with whom he was frequently associated. His debt to Impressionism, however, was real. A critic in a review of the 1931 Schofield exhibition at the Corcoran Gallery of Art formulated it this way: "At the time that Mr. Schofield studied in Paris the French Impressionist school was at its height, and doubtless he profited by the contact, but he never employed the French impressionists' methods, and he always painted with a full brush, broadly. He did learn, however, either from the French impressionists or because the problems of light were uppermost in everyone's mind at that time, how to interpret truly effects of sunlight and air with astounding realism" (*The Star* [Washington, D.C.], October 25, 1931). In *McLegrenow Farm* this mastery in representing light and atmosphere is especially evident.

Ex coll.:
Sale, Sotheby Parke-Bernet, Inc., New York, October 27, 1978, no. 162; Dr. and Mrs. John J. McDonough, Youngstown, Ohio.

McLegrenow Farm
1920

oil on canvas
30 x 36 in. (76.2 x 91.4 cm.)
Signed and dated, lower left: Schofield '20

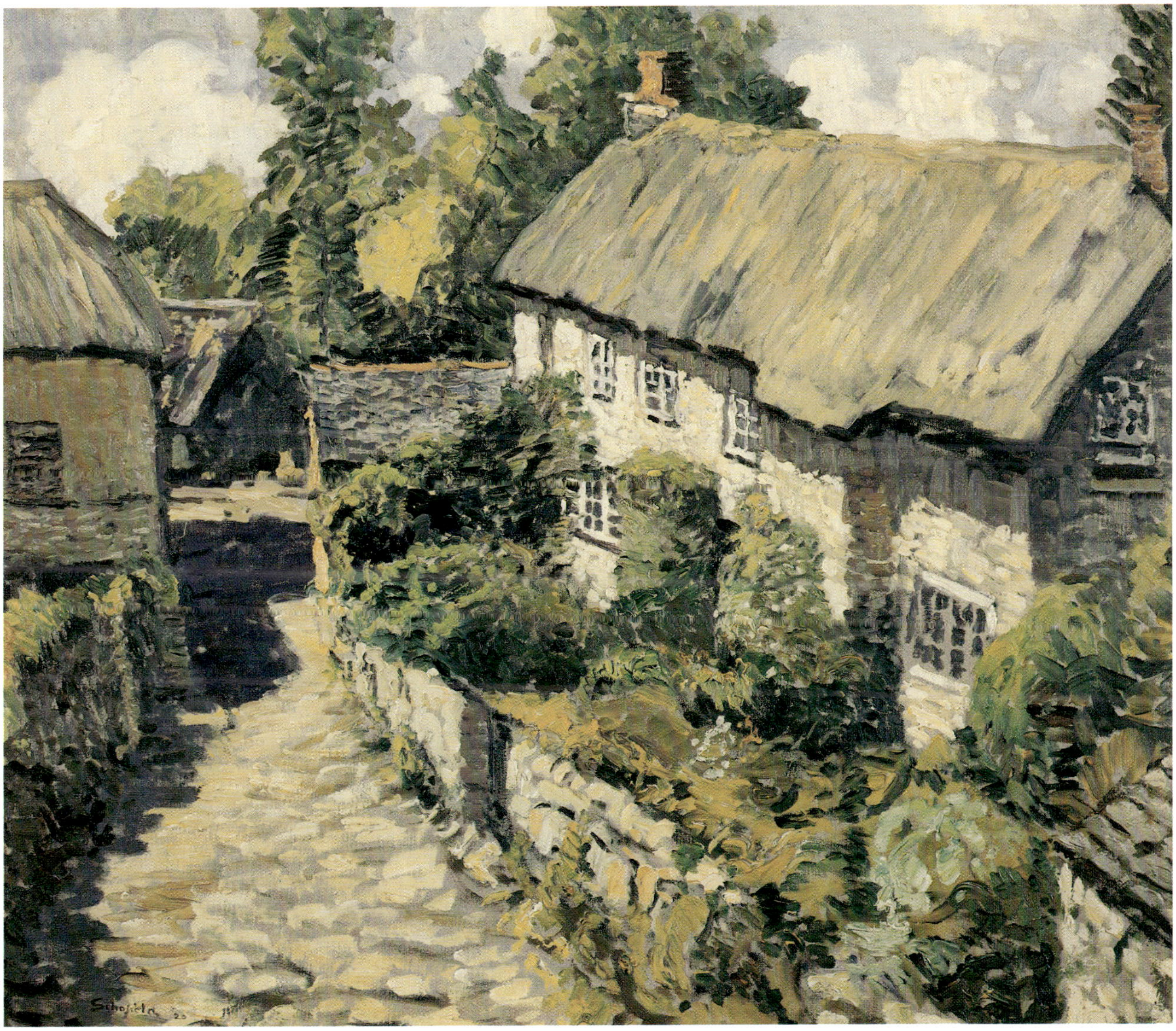

Edward Emerson Simmons
(1852-1931)

The original title of this unusual work by Simmons is unknown, but it most likely represents a scene of fishermen on the Brittany coast. Simmons lived in this area of France, at the village of Concarneau, from 1881 through 1886, and frequently painted scenes showing the local inhabitants in their traditional attire. Here, the fishermen seem to be singing or making music at the same time that they are inspecting or repairing a fishing net. The baskets used as containers for the fish are also part of the scene, but they appear to be empty.

During his years in France, Simmons, who in later years became almost exclusively a muralist, painted many genre scenes with large figures but seldom attempted landscape. In this work, which for all practical purposes is a landscape, he did so in a manner that seems rather American and calls to mind the seascapes of American Luminist painters such as John F. Kensett and Sanford Robinson Gifford. A low horizon line, a panoramic view, and a sense of infinite visibility were elements of the Luminist style, and served Simmons well in depicting this scene on the Brittany coast. In this respect a typically caustic comment made by Simmons in his autobiography is of interest: "The British artists passed by Concarneau and went on to Pont Aven where there were ready-made landscapes for the watercolorists. Truth to tell, they were frightened by the bigness of the coast and left it to the French and Americans, who formed a very happy crowd" (Edward Simmons, *From Seven to Seventy* [1922], p. 145).

Ex coll.:
Sale, Butterfield and Butterfield, Inc., San Francisco, October 8, 1980, no. 136; Dr. and Mrs. John J. McDonough, Youngstown, Ohio.

Figures on a Beach
1882

oil on canvas
18¼ x 24 in. (46.4 x 61 cm.)
Signed and dated, lower right: E. E. Simmons 82

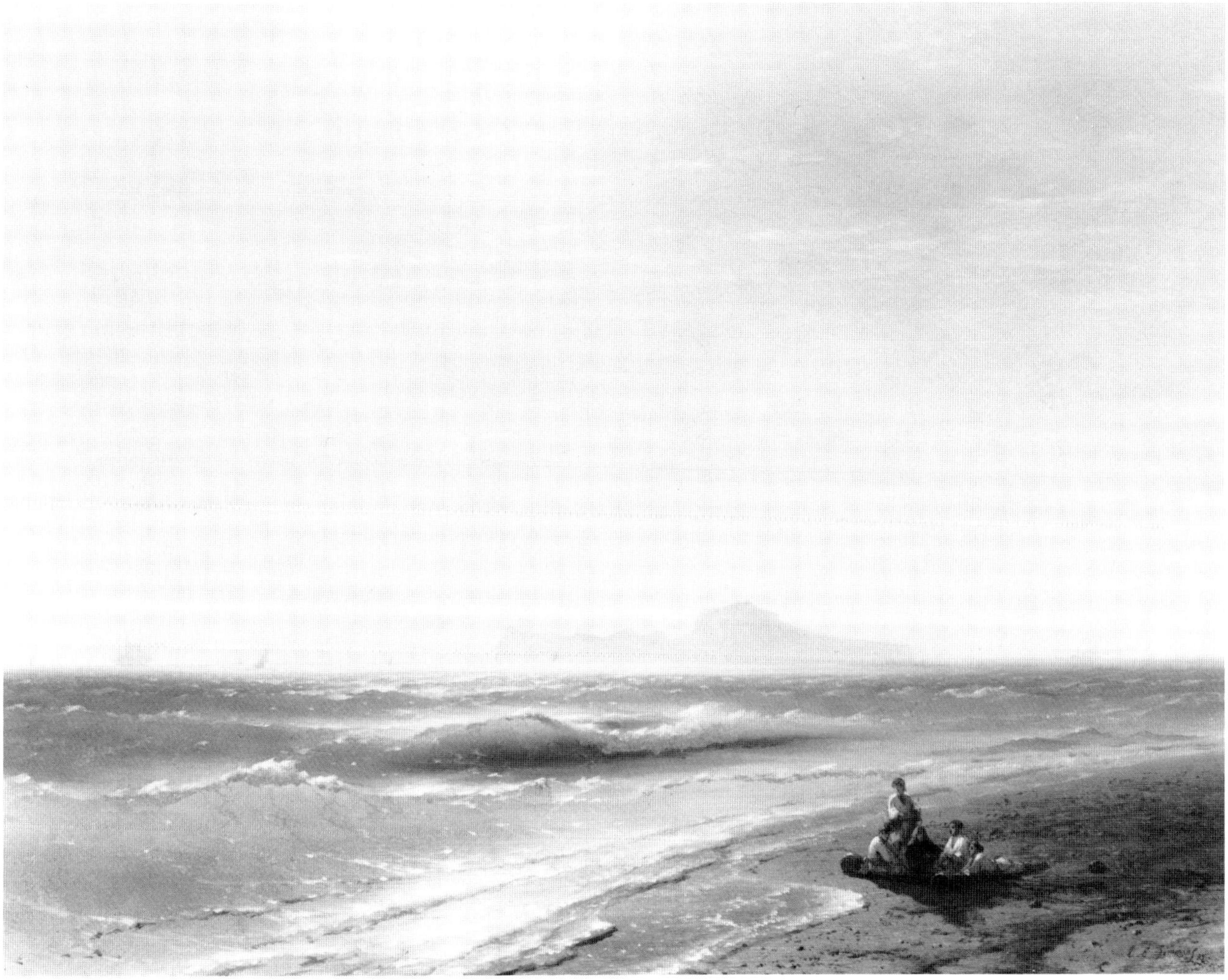

George Gardner Symons
(1861?-1930)

Although Gardner Symons was best known during his lifetime for his New England winter landscapes and for his California scenes, it is known that he traveled and painted abroad throughout most of his career. One of the places he visited more than once was Cornwall, in England, where his friend Walter Schofield lived. He was certainly there for a number of years between 1900 and 1906, chiefly in the village of St. Ives on the coast, and probably intermittently until about 1915, after which time the number of English scenes in his exhibitions dramatically diminishes. This work, revealing in its lively colorism the great appeal the little village of St. Ives long held for British and American artists, was probably painted during Symons's early years in Cornwall, perhaps about 1905. Its execution is entirely competent and assured, but it is looser and more impressionistic than Symons's style of about 1910 and after. It must be admitted, however, that Symons's paintings have not been adequately studied and that this dating is tentative.

In 1916, a year after this work was exhibited at the Pratt Institute in Brooklyn, a critic quoted this apt characterization of Symons's style: "You might call him a realist, for he is one; vigorous, direct, clear-cut; or an impressionist, for light and air are put into his canvases to stay. But there is something more besides the robustness, besides the fine color and glittering light; it is a sort of inside principle, informing his work and creating its special character, a broadness, a joyousness, a hopefulness, a certain wide-eyed jubilant outlook. You find yourself compelled to note the temperament and the secure and blithe handling together, and you have no choice but to call him an optimist in Art" (Thomas Shrewsbury Parkhurst, "Gardner Symons—Painter and Philosopher," *The Fine Arts Journal* 34 [November 1916], p. 564).

Exhibited:
Art Gallery, Pratt Institute, Brooklyn, New York, 1915, *Exhibition of Twenty Three Landscape Paintings by Gardner Symons*, no. 5.

Ex coll.:
Estate of the artist; Zara Symons Betts; estate of Irene Treverrow, Bronxville, New York; sale, Sotheby Parke-Bernet, Inc., New York, January 30, 1980, no. 295; Dr. and Mrs. John J. McDonough, Youngstown, Ohio.

Fishing Village, St. Ives
c. 1900-15

oil on canvas
25 x 30 in. (63.5 x 76.2 cm.)
Signed, lower left: Gardner Symons

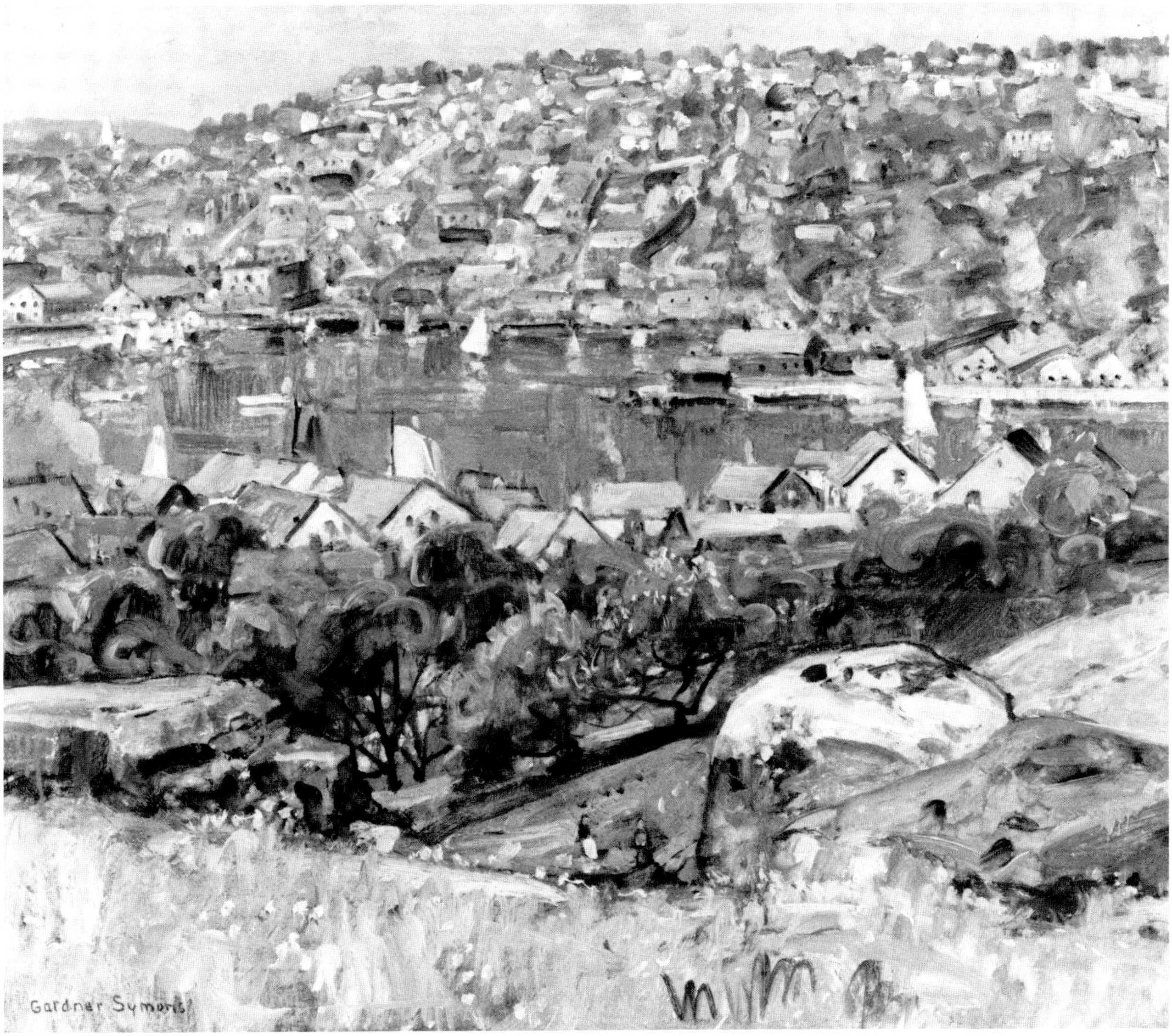

John Henry Twachtman
(1853-1902)

In 1889 Twachtman purchased a farmhouse and seventeen acres of land on Round Hill Road, about two miles from Greenwich, Connecticut. This property contained a number of buildings as well as a pond, waterfall, and stream known, respectively, as Hemlock Pool, Horseneck Falls, and Horseneck Brook. They provided a seemingly inexhaustible source of inspiration for Twachtman, and he painted them repeatedly in different seasons and at different times of the day (Richard J. Boyle, *John Twachtman* [1979], p. 65). *Winter Landscape with Stream* is part of this series of works and represents substantially the same view as *End of Winter* (after 1889, National Museum of American Art, Washington, D.C.).

Probably the most individual of the American painters who studied in France and were influenced by Impressionism, Twachtman developed a style that is more Tonalist than Impressionist in technique, though, to be sure, it is a style that is inconceivable without Monet. In his snow-covered winter scenes, in particular, the individuality of his approach reveals itself. In these, Twachtman's disregard for analytic observation, his vigorous and labored execution, and his concern for creating a mood, rather than re-creating a visual experience, are readily apparent. He articulated this mood in a letter to his good friend and Connecticut neighbor, Julian Alden Weir: "Never is nature more lovely than when it is snowing. Everything is so quiet and the whole earth seems wrapped in a mantle. . . . All nature is hushed to silence" (quoted in William H. Gerdts, *American Impressionism* [1980], p. 68).

References:
Steven Straw Company, Inc., Newburyport, Massachusetts, *American Selections 1978* (1978), unpaged, ill. in color.

Exhibited:
Indian Hill Historical Museum Association, Cincinnati, Ohio, 1978, *The Golden Era of Art*, no. 79.

Ex coll.:
Private collection, Ireland; Ira Spanierman, Inc., New York; Steven Straw Company, Inc., Newburyport, Massachusetts, until 1978; Dr. and Mrs. John J. McDonough, Youngstown, Ohio.

Winter Landscape with Stream
c. 1895

oil on canvas
22 x 28 in. (55.9 x 71.1 cm.)
Signed, lower left: J.H. Twachtman

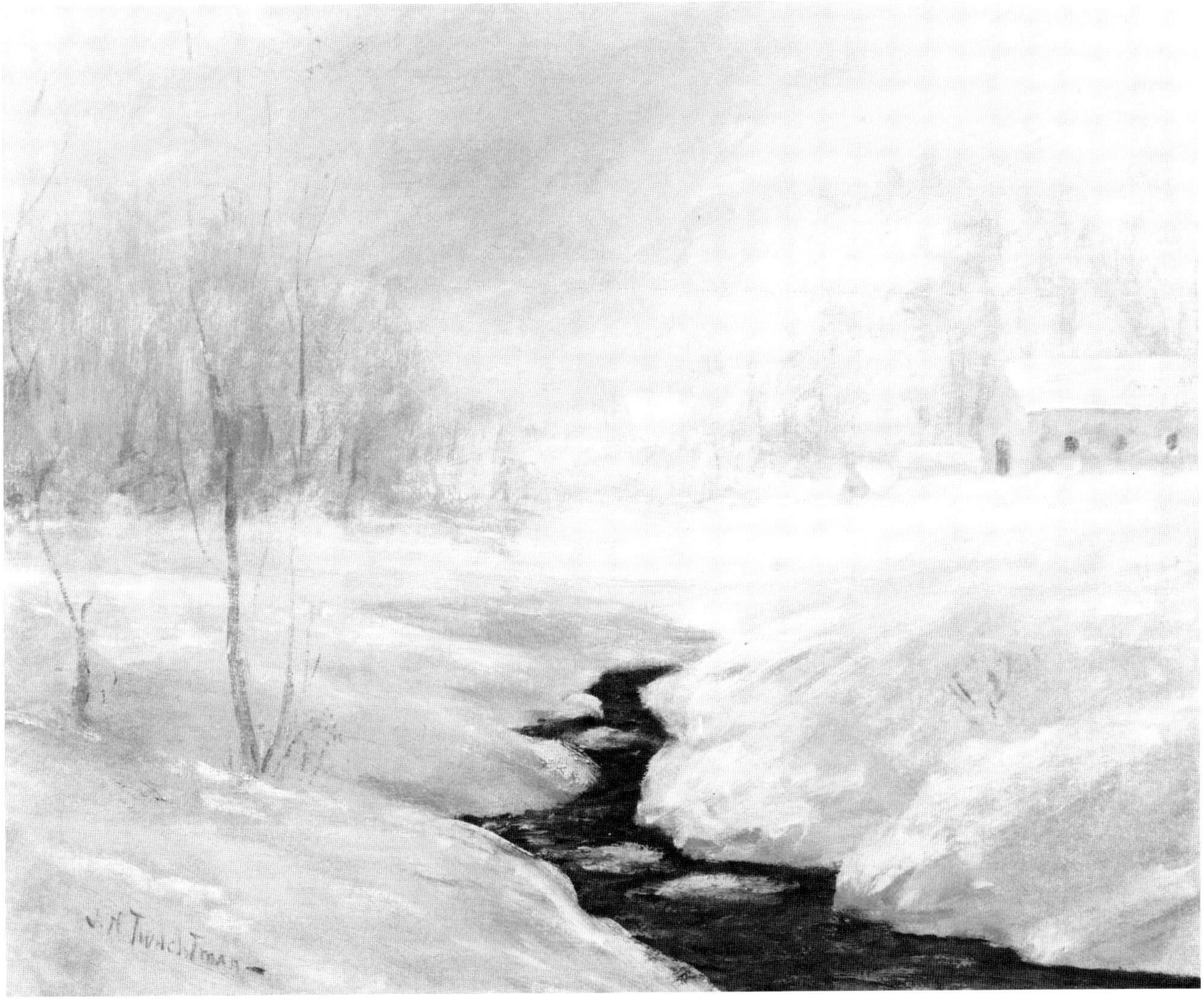

Robert William Vonnoh
(1858-1933)

Vonnoh developed an interest in landscape painting during his stay in France between 1887 and 1891. Though he was clearly influenced by Impressionism, the cool, silvery tonality of his works, their restrained brushwork, and their well thought out composition clearly reveal a debt to Corot and to Jules Bastien-Lepage. He also experimented a good deal on his own, as this painting, almost exclusively executed with a palette knife, clearly demonstrates. In a letter to John Dorr Bradley of Chicago, who purchased the work after seeing it at an exhibition at the Art Institute, Vonnoh wrote: "I call it Moist Weather (France). It was painted in 1890, or a little before at Grez Sur Loing-Seine et Marne; where I have a little country place. I considered it one of the most successful things that I had done, & it was shown in several of my Exhs around that period. It did not sell, as it is not of the popular sort of picture. I had compliments from artists on this canvas, & got to rather like to have it about. I therefore kept it hanging in my home all these years. Lately I reframed it and sent it to several Exhs with the result that it was still much liked by the artists. Doubtless, if this miserable war had not knocked out all my summers work in France, I should have had pictures enough to fill my Exhs, so that this is perhaps the main reason that "Moist Weather" (France), has found a home at last" (Vonnoh to John Dorr Bradley, December 3, 1915).

References:
Robert Vonnoh, letter to John Dorr Bradley, December 3, 1915, ms. in possession of Dr. John J. McDonough, Youngstown, Ohio.

Exhibited:
Rochester, New York, *Rochester Exposition*, 1914; Art Institute of Chicago, 1915.

Ex coll.:
The artist, until 1915; John Dorr Bradley, Chicago; sale, Sotheby Parke-Bernet, Inc., New York, April 20, 1979, no. 79; Dr. and Mrs. John J. McDonough, Youngstown, Ohio.

Moist Weather (France)
1890

oil on canvas
25½ x 21¼ in. (64.8 x 54 cm.)
Signed and dated, lower left: Vonnoh, 1890

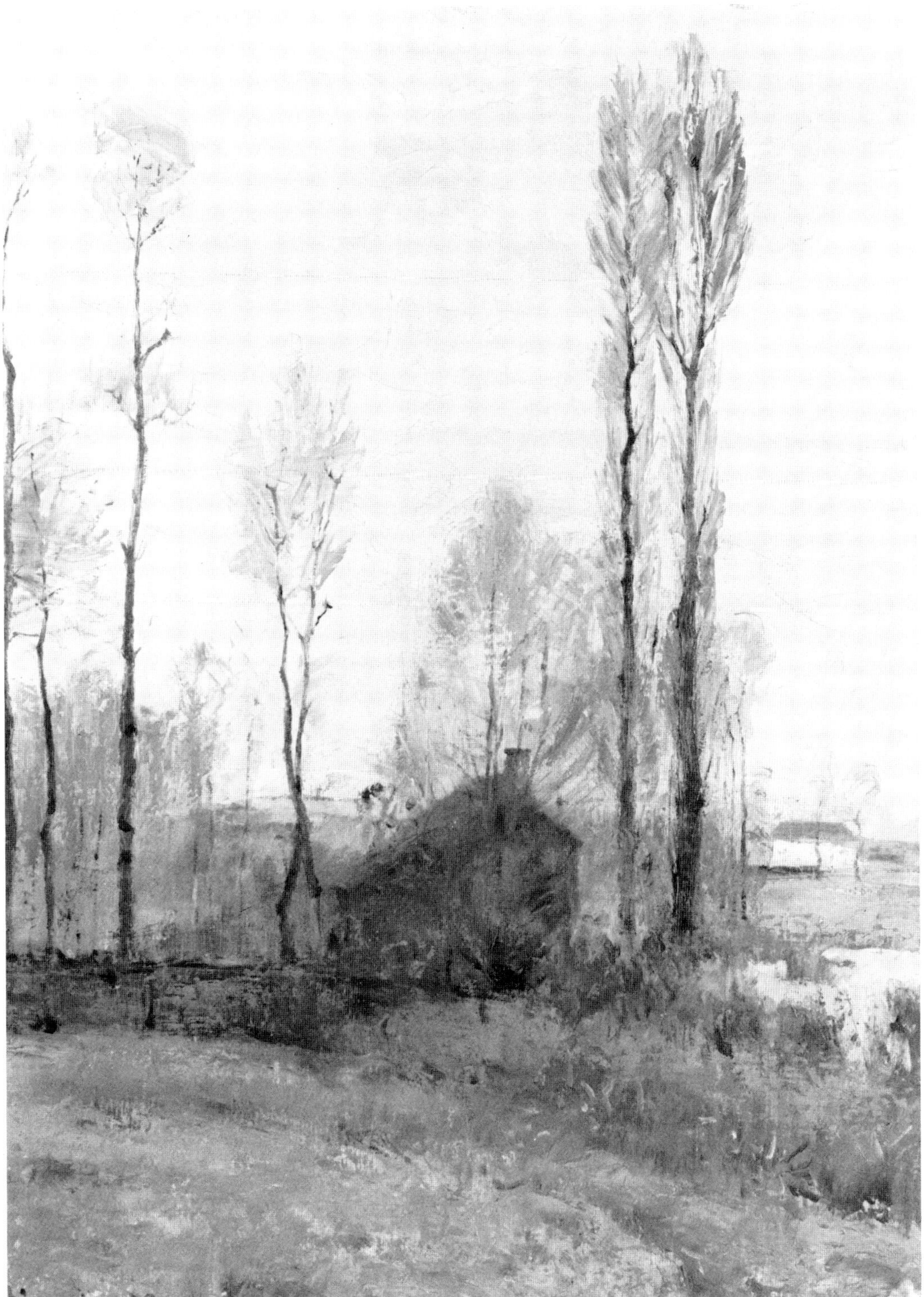

Robert William Vonnoh
(1858-1933)

On the back of a photograph of this work, Vonnoh identified it as having been painted in Pleasant Valley, Lyme, Connecticut where he owned a house and studio, four or five years before July 1921, when he actually wrote the inscription (photograph in collection of Dr. and Mrs. John J. McDonough). This documentation is of particular significance because, though it is known that Vonnoh frequented the artists' colony at Lyme after about 1905, few of his works painted there have been identified.

During his later years, Vonnoh led a more or less dual artistic life. As a portrait painter, he practiced a realistic, highly academic style, while as a landscape painter he was committed to Impressionism. From 1891 until 1896 he taught portrait-painting at the Pennsylvania Academy of the Fine Arts, but it is clear that his influence on students such as Elmer Schofield, Edward Redfield, John Sloan, and Robert Henri went beyond portraiture. Vonnoh was an effective promoter of Impressionism and, as a progressive force, was much admired by his students. At Lyme, he occupied the same position amidst a group of younger artists.

Compared to Vonnoh's earlier work in this exhibition, *Early Spring* displays a fuller understanding of Impressionist technique, though the silvery tones of Corot are still present in the sky. The pure bits of color placed next to each other in the foreground reveal the influence Monet exercised on his art after about 1888 and are typical of the vibrant color and brushwork of his mature landscapes.

References:
Robert W. Vonnoh, note on back of a photograph, ms. in collection of Dr. and Mrs. John J. McDonough, gives title of painting, identifies date and place of execution, and notes: "July 1921/Pleasant Valley, Lyme Conn./painted about 4 or 5 yrs. ago./A pastoral Landscape/and a poets [sic] day/One could but reflect,/at least, some of the/charm of such a time/and place-/Robert Vonnoh"

Ex coll.:
The artist, until about 1921; M.A. Newhouse and Son, St. Louis, Missouri, 1921; Kuno H. Struck, Davenport, Iowa; sale, Sotheby Parke-Bernet, Inc., New York, April 21, 1978, no. 76; Dr. and Mrs. John J. McDonough, Youngstown, Ohio.

Early Spring
c. 1916-17

oil on canvas
24 x 30 in. (61 x 76.2 cm.)
Signed, lower right: Vonnoh

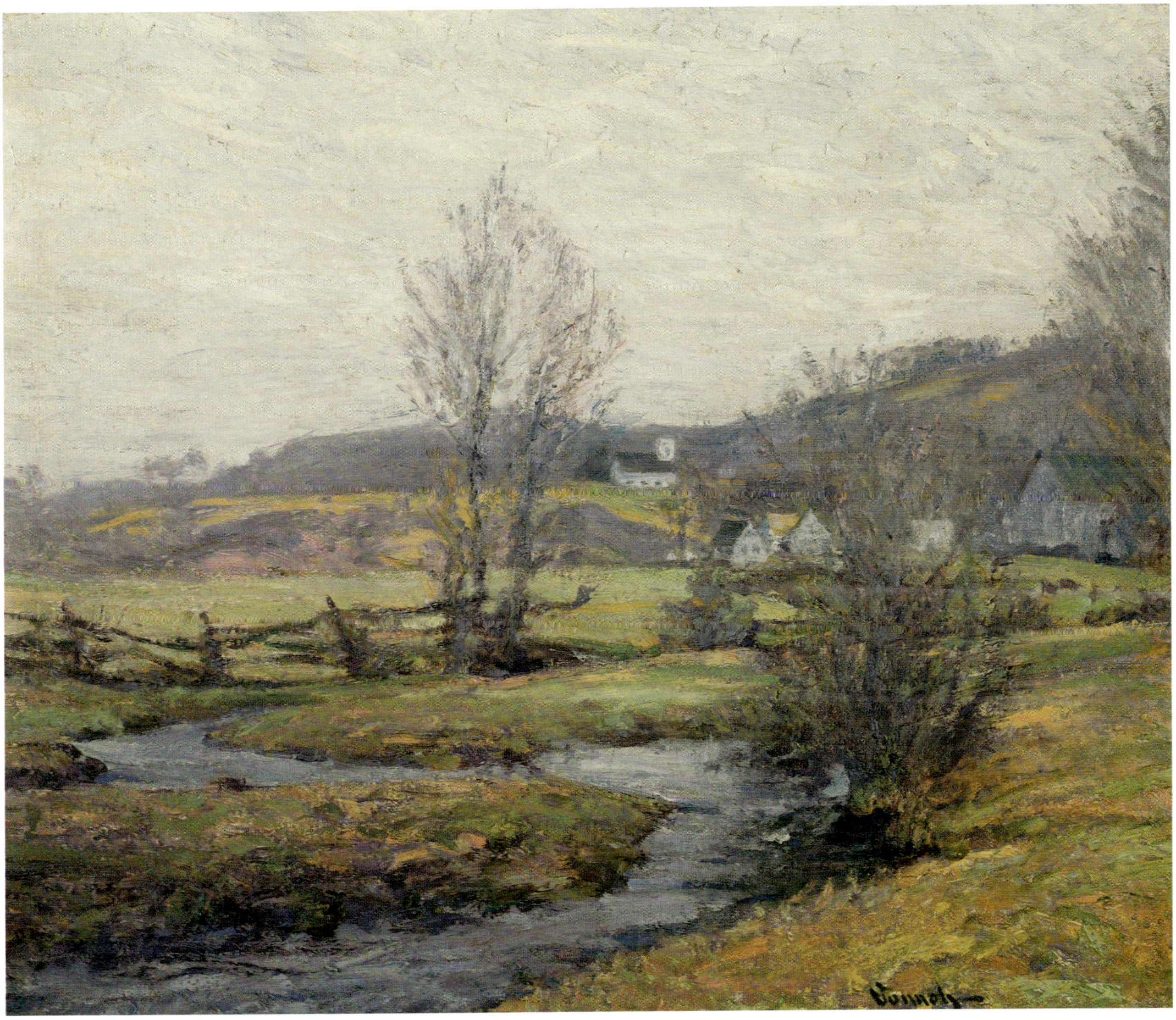

Julian Alden Weir
(1852-1919)

As a student in Europe between 1873 and 1877, Weir was exposed to Impressionism but decided he wanted no part of it. He placed himself firmly in the traditional academic camp, though after trips to Holland and Spain he developed a great admiration for the works of Hals and Velázquez. After seeing the third Impressionist exhibition in Paris in 1877, he referred to it as a "Chamber of Horrors" and on April 15 of that year wrote his parents: "They do not observe drawing or form but give you an impression of what they call nature" (quoted in Dorothy Weir Young, *The Life and Letters of J. Alden Weir* [1960], p. 123).

In time, however, Weir became persuaded of the validity of Impressionist aims and changed his style accordingly. This great transformation in his work occurred in the decade of the 1890s, but before that the artist had become an admirer of Manet's still life paintings and had produced many such works in the French master's painterly, sensuous manner. These were much admired by Weir's patrons and artist friends. In 1924, William A. Coffin, summarizing Weir's achievements on the occasion of the Weir Memorial Exhibition at the Metropolitan Museum of Art noted: "Strong emphasis must be laid on the beauty of his still life pictures: roses, generally white, in bowls; silver, china and glass with them; occasionally tulips, sometimes fruits. He was painting these in the eighties and no survey of his painting would be complete without giving them prominence. They are interpretations of compelling charm, technically subtle, distinguished in color, never aggressive, possessing simplicity and restraint, always beautiful" (Metropolitan Museum of Art, New York, 1924, *Memorial Exhibition of the Works of Julian Alden Weir*, pp. xv-xvi).

References:
Peter H. Davidson, letter to Dr. John J. McDonough, January 5, 1982, notes: "your Weir still-life appears as #A122 on page five of the Mahonri Young Estate Inventory, which was prepared by M. Knoedler & Co. It is listed as 'Vase & Roses'."

Ex coll.:
Estate of the artist; his daughter, Dorothy Weir Young; her husband Mahonri M. Young, New York, until 1957; his son, Mahonri Sharp Young, until about 1958; Brigham Young University, Provo, Utah; Tivoli Gallery, Salt Lake City, Utah; sale, Sotheby Parke-Bernet, Inc., New York, May 29, 1981, no. 1; Dr. and Mrs. John J. McDonough, Youngstown, Ohio.

Vase and Roses
c. 1882-90

oil on canvas
12 x 14 in. (30.5 x 35.6 cm.)

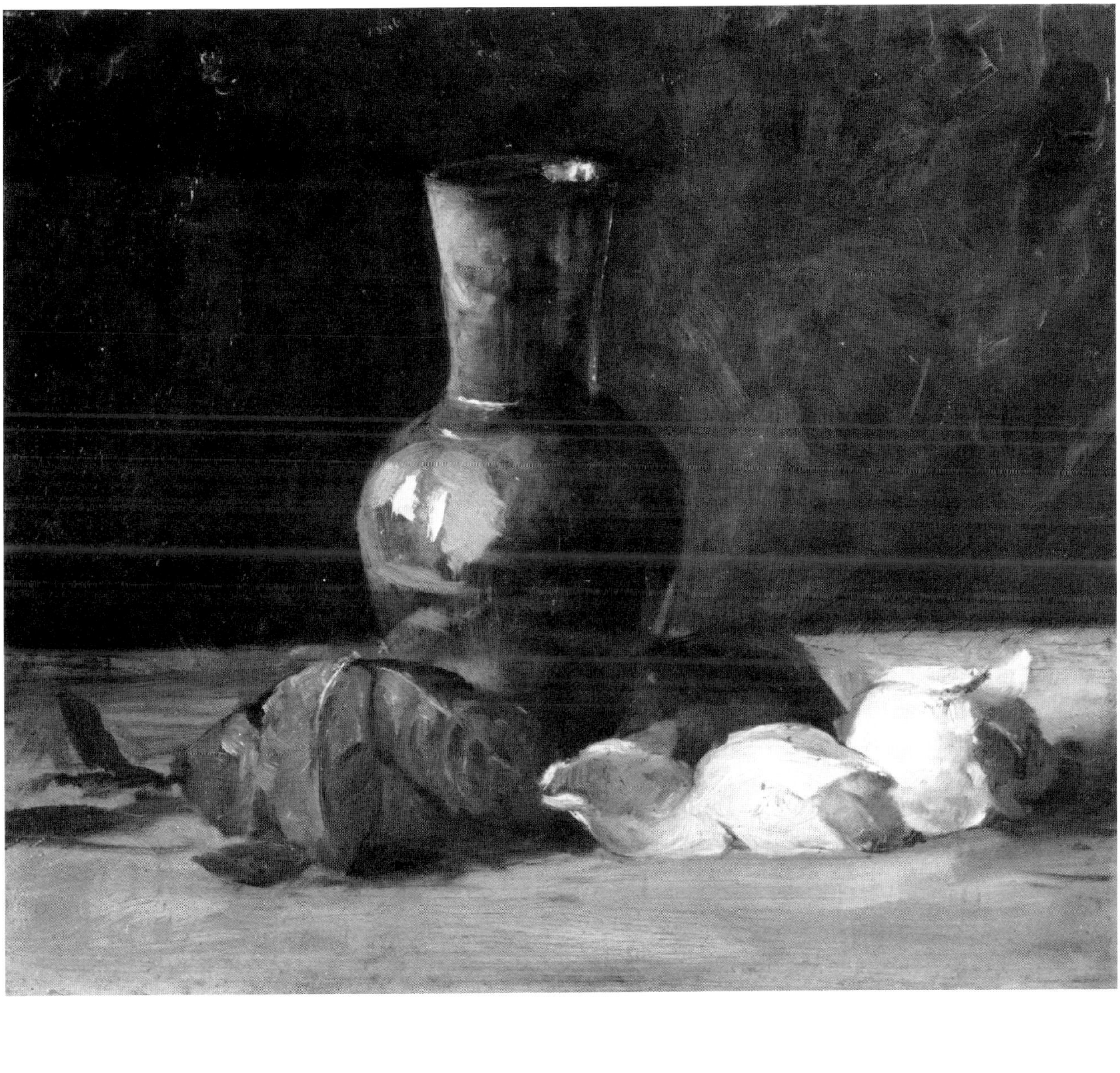

Julian Alden Weir
(1852-1919)

In the decade of the 1890s, Julian Alden Weir began to experiment with the light palette and broken brushwork associated with Impressionism. His style eventually became one of high-keyed color applied in small thin strokes. It was not a free, painterly style but rather one calculated to define shapes clearly while at the same time conveying a lively sense of color and producing a rich surface.

Most of Weir's landscapes, including this work, were painted in Branchville, Connecticut, where he owned two farms. The collector Duncan Phillips, an admirer of Weir's work, accurately described these paintings as follows: "In the pictures painted on his two Connecticut farms there is a monotony of contentment. A drowsy, quivering heat pervades the air. The sun silvers the woods beyond the rocky pastures. If only one could paint the hum of insect life and of incidental, unimportant human voices, the sensation of a summer's day on a farm, to one dreaming in the grass, would be complete" (Duncan Phillips, *A Collection in the Making* [1926], p. 40).

This painting has gone under a number of titles in the past, including *Upland Pasture*, *Cattle in the Birches*, and *Autumn*. It is clear from family records, however, that it was originally known as *The Birches*.

References:
Laura Morse (Mrs. Charles H.) Bayley, letter to Dorothy Weir Young, October 20, 1926, in possession of the artist's family, states that her husband purchased the picture from the artist after it was exhibited at the Boston Art Club and notes that "we consider it an especially fine example of your father's work"; Dorothy Weir Young, "Records of the Paintings of J. Alden Weir," 4, pp. 288-288A, provides provenance and exhibitions, says it was purchased by C.H. Bayley on February 3, 1903 and gives title as *The Birches*; *Antiques* 118 (November 1980), p. 804, ill. in color as *Upland Pasture*.

Exhibited:
Boston Art Club, Boston, 1904, *65th Exhibition*, no. 61, as *Upland Pasture*, lent by C.H. Bayley; Museum of Fine Arts, Boston, 1911, on deposit, as *Autumn*, lent by C.H. Bayley; Lowe Art Museum, University of Miami, Coral Gables, Florida, 1971, *French Impressionsts Influence American Artists*, no. 189, as *Upland Pasture*, lent by Schweitzer Gallery, New York; Queens Museum, Flushing, New York, 1976, *Cows*, no. 71, as *Upland Pasture*.

Ex coll.:
Charles H. Bayley, Boston; Dr. and Mrs. Jansen, Hoornbeeck, Vermont; Schweitzer Gallery, Inc., New York, 1971; private collection, Wellesley, Massachusetts; Vose Galleries, Inc., Boston, 1980; Dr. and Mrs. John J. McDonough, Youngstown, Ohio.

The Birches
1903

oil on canvas
34¼ x 27¼ in. (87 x 69.2 cm.)
Signed and dated, lower left: J. Alden Weir 1903

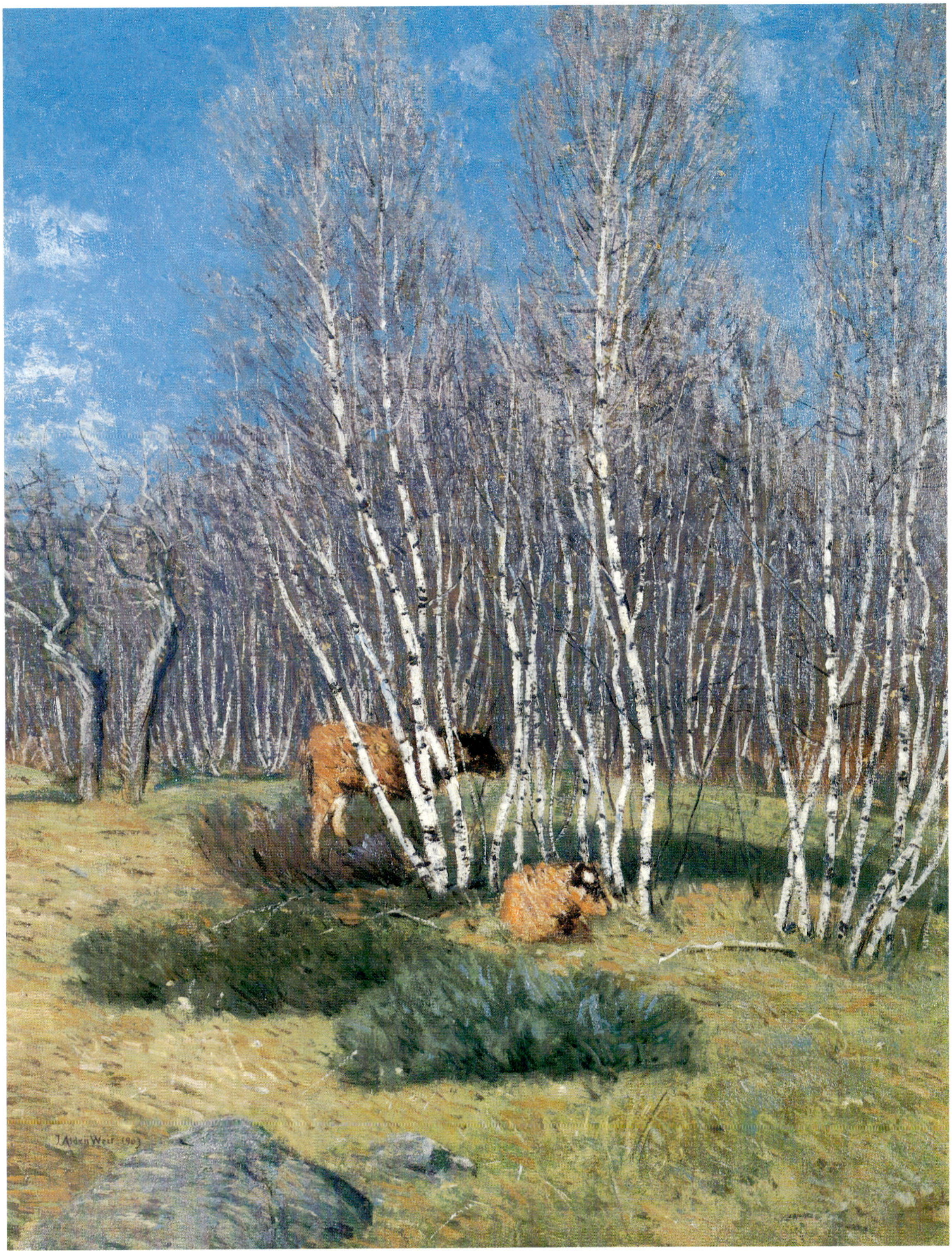

Theodore Wendel
(1859-1932)

One of the first American artists to meet Monet and to be influenced by him, Theodore Wendel painted landscapes and townscapes in Europe and America, concentrating after 1899 on views painted in and around Ipswich, Massachusetts. Wendel's wife had inherited a large farm in Ipswich from her father, the wealthy Asa Pease Stone, and, until his death in 1932, the painter lived there. Although prior to 1900 Wendel's work, primarily urban scenes of Boston, possessed impressionist qualities, it was not until his move to Ipswich that he arrived at a highly individual and recognizable style. As John I.H. Baur, the leading student of Wendel's art, has noted, it is the Ipswich paintings that combine the intimate poetic quality of his early work in Giverny with a new brilliance of light and color that is peculiarly American: "These pictures, though subtle, are full of the sparkle of a New England summer day" (John I.H. Baur, "Introducing Theodore Wendel," *Art in America* 64 [November-December, 1976], p. 105).

Executed in the vicinity of Ipswich, *Lady with Parasol by Stream* (the title given the work by Wendel's son Daniel Wendel) actually depicts two ladies either returning from, or about to go, boating on a placid stream. This subject was a favorite one with French and American Impressionists. Here Wendel, employing a straightforward panoramic composition and applying his pigments in flat, deliberate strokes, has interpreted the theme in a quiet way, reminiscent of Hudson River School formulas.

References:
Antiques 116 (August 1979), p. 212, ill. in color.

Ex coll.:
The artist's son, Daniel Wendel, Ipswich, Massachusetts, until 1979; Vose Galleries, Inc., Boston, 1979; Dr. and Mrs. John J. McDonough, Youngstown, Ohio.

Lady with Parasol by Stream
c. 1905-15

oil on canvas c. 1905-1915
20 x 30 in. (50.8 x 76.2 cm.)

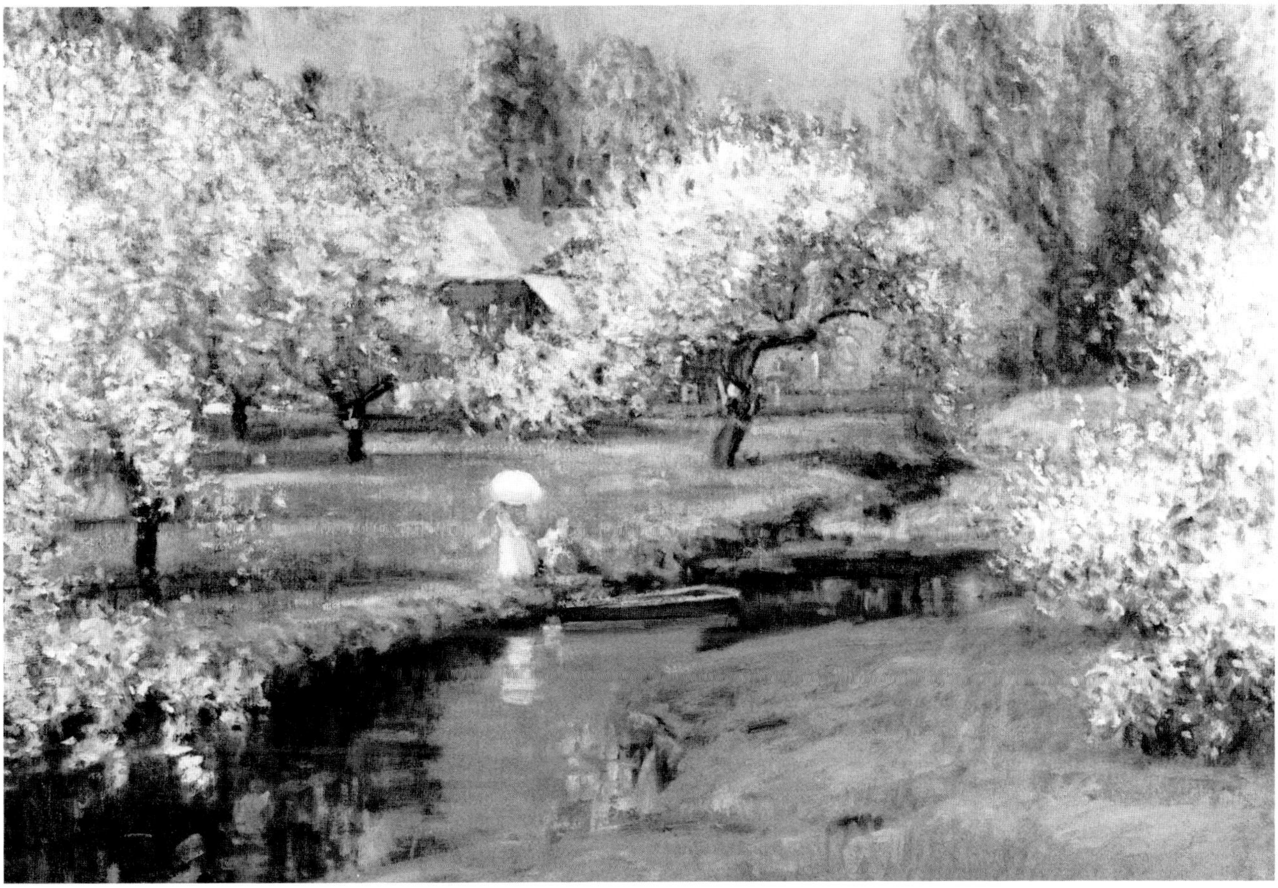

John Whorf
(1903-1959)

For most of his career as a watercolorist, Whorf was regarded as the worthy successor of Winslow Homer and John Singer Sargent. He was associated with Homer in that he often dealt with marine subject matter, but his technique was closer to Sargent's. In a review of his 1929 one-man exhibition at the Milch Galleries in New York, this association was noted: "Collectors of Sargent watercolors who buy them for something more than the master's name should be grateful to John Whorf. He has carried on that part of the Sargent tradition in a highly competent manner, not in the role of copyist but in that of student and admirer. His color is brilliant and hard and has excellent black and white value; his technique is that of a virtuoso. The dramatic quality of his illustrations of tempestuous life on sea and shore is sometimes more stressed than was usual with Sargent but may constitute an added attraction. A few of his pictures might very well relieve the monotony of the famous Sargent corridor in the Boston Museum" ("Exhibitions in the New York Galleries, " *Art News* 27 [April 13, 1929], pp. 11, 14).

Whorf frequently painted scenes in Gloucester. A number of works depicting the town proper, the harbor, and the activities along the piers and wharves are known. Although this work was executed long after 1925, it is included in this exhibition because Whorf's style is so closely allied with early 20th-century American Impressionism.

Ex coll.:
Sale, Sotheby Parke-Bernet, Inc. (PB 84), New York, February 21, 1978, no. 200; Dr. and Mrs. John J. McDonough, Youngstown, Ohio.

Foggy Morning in Gloucester
1953

watercolor on paper
21 x 30 in. (53.3 x 76.2 cm.)
Signed and dated, lower right: John Whorf 53
Inscribed, on back: This picture has never been properly shown and I think it is one of my best.

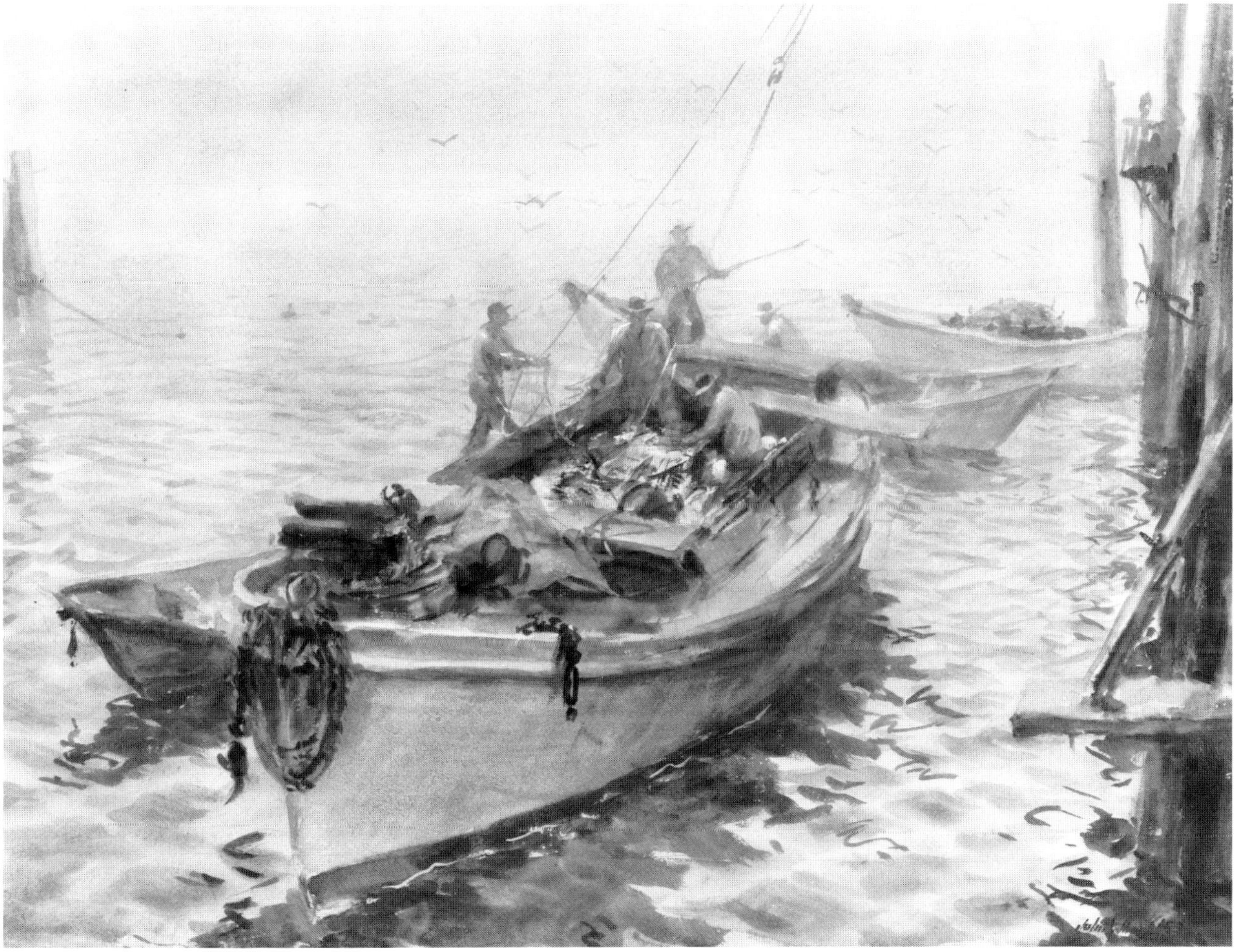

BIOGRAPHIES

Bellows, George
(1882-1925)

Bellows grew up in Columbus, Ohio, and attended Ohio State University. He went against his family's wishes in deciding to become an artist and never graduated. In 1904 he enrolled at the New York School of Art where he studied with Kenneth Hayes Miller and Robert Henri (q.v.), whose circle he joined, becoming a devoted follower. An artist of great facility, he was included in the 1907 National Academy of Design exhibition. In 1908 he received the Hallgarten Second Prize and in 1909 was elected an associate member of the Academy. From 1910 to 1911 he taught the life class at the Art Students' League. In 1913 he was made a full member of the N.A.D. and participated in the Armory Show. His works enjoyed great popularity from the start, especially his urban scenes, but he also concentrated on landscapes during summer trips. His wife and two daughters (born 1911 and 1915) were frequent subjects of his portraits. He died in New York City where he had mostly lived since leaving Ohio.

Bunker, Dennis Miller
(1861-1890)

Born in New York, Bunker attended art classes at the National Academy of Design and the Art Students' League, at the latter under William Merritt Chase (q.v.). He first exhibited at the N.A.D. in 1880. In 1882 he went to Paris where he studied under Antoine-Auguste-Ernest Hébert at the Académie Julian and under Jean-Léon Gérôme at the Ecole des Beaux-Arts. Bunker spent summers in the French countryside and produced works influenced by the Barbizon school as well as by the Impressionists. Returning to the United States in 1885, after a brief time in New York he settled in Boston where he taught at the Cowles Art School, was befriended by Isabella Stewart Gardner, and circulated in high society. Most of his work at this time consisted of academic-style portraits. In 1887 he met John Singer Sargent (q.v.) in Boston and in 1888 spent time with him in England. From this time on, his landscapes showed the brilliant colors and loose brushwork of Sargent. In 1889 he moved to New York in search of portrait commissions which did not materialize. In October 1890, in poor health and in financial straits, he married Eleanor Hardy of Boston. A few months later, while in that city for the Christmas holidays, he died of heart failure.

Butler, Theodore Earl
(1860-1936)

Born in Columbus, Ohio, Butler attended Marietta College from 1876 to 1880. He went to New York in 1882 and studied at the Art Students' League. By 1885 he was in Paris where he studied at the Académie Julian, at the Atelier Colarossi, and at the Grande Chaumière. He was represented at the Paris Salon of 1888 and won an Honorable Mention. That summer he was taken to meet Claude Monet at Giverny by Theodore Robinson (q.v.). Henceforth, Butler's style was an impressionist one closely derived from Monet's. He returned to America in 1890, but by the end of the following year he was back at Giverny. In 1892 he married Suzanne Hoschedé, daughter of Monet's second wife. Some years after her death in 1899, he married her sister Marthe Hoschedé. He returned to the United States in 1899 and the next year arranged for an exhibition of his work at Durand-Ruel, New York. Between 1900 and 1913 he lived at Giverny; he is said to have painted mural decorations for the United States Pavilion at the 1911 Turin International Exposition. Butler was in America between 1914 and 1921 and befriended John Sloan. In 1917 he helped found the Society of Independent Artists in New York. In 1921 he returned to Giverny where he spent the last fifteen years of his life.

Cassatt, Mary Stevenson (1844-1926)

Cassatt was born in Allegheny City, Pennsylvania, now part of Pittsburgh. While still a child she moved to Philadelphia where she studied at the Pennsylvania Academy of the Fine Arts in 1864 and 1865. In 1866 she went to Europe to travel and study the Old Masters. She settled in Paris in 1868 and studied there independently and under Benjamin Constant. She also studied at the Royal Academy in Parma, Italy, in 1872. Between 1872 and 1876 she had paintings accepted in the Paris Salon. In 1877 she was invited by Edgar Degas to exhibit with the Impressionists. She continued to exhibit with them until 1886 and increasingly came under Degas's influence. In 1891 she had her first one-artist show at Durand-Ruel in Paris. In 1892 she painted mural decorations for the World's Columbian Exposition in Chicago. In 1914 she was awarded the Gold Medal of Honor by the Pennsylvania Academy. In addition to her work, her importance lies in the interest she generated among American collectors in the work of the Impressionists.

Chase, William Merritt (1849-1916)

Born in Williamsburg, Indiana, Chase first studied portrait painting in 1867 under Benjamin F. Hayes in Indianapolis. In 1869 he went to New York where he studied with L. E. Wilmarth at the National Academy of Design until 1871. He then joined his parents in St. Louis. With the financial help of local patrons, he was sent to Germany in 1872 to study at the Royal Academy in Munich. There he studied with Alexander Wagner and Karl von Piloty. He was chiefly influenced, however, by the dark realism of Wilhelm Leibl and his group. While there he met the American painter Frank Duveneck. Before returning to America in 1878 he spent nine months in Venice with him and John Henry Twachtman (q.v.). In 1876 he was awarded a medal for painting at the Philadelphia Centennial Exposition for a work sent from abroad. Back in New York he became a teacher at the newly-formed Art Students' League and joined the Society of American Artists. Between 1881 and 1885 he made trips to Spain and Holland. In 1891 he established a summer art school at Shinnecock on Long Island. In 1896 he opened his own school in New York City where he taught until 1908. He joined the Ten American Painters group in 1902, and his first one-man show took place at M. Knoedler and Co. in New York in 1903. In 1904 he won the Gold Medal for painting at the St. Louis Exposition.

Cornoyer, Paul (1864-1923)

Born in St. Louis, Missouri, Cornoyer received his early training at the St. Louis Art School where he was encouraged by its director, Halsey C. Ives. In 1889 he left for Paris to study at the Académie Julian. There he received a sound academic training, but it was the works of the Impressionists that influenced him most. He returned to St. Louis in 1894. Shortly thereafter he sent a painting for exhibition at the Pennsylvania Academy of the Fine Arts, which was purchased by William Merritt Chase (q.v.). In 1898, at Chase's urging, he moved to New York where he met the leading American Impressionists. In 1904 he became a member of the Salmagundi Club and in 1906 won the Inness Prize awarded by it. In 1908 he was given a one-man show by the Albright Art Gallery in Buffalo, New York; in 1909 he became an associate of the National Academy of Design. Cornoyer mostly painted city scenes in New York throughout his active career. He also had a summer house in Gloucester, Massachusetts, however, and many of his works are views of its area.

Curran, Charles Courtney (1861-1942)

Curran was born in Hartford, Kentucky, but was raised in Norwalk, Ohio. He first studied art at the Cincinnati School of Design. About 1879 he was in New York where he studied at the National Academy of Design and the Art Students' League. Some years later he was in Paris at the Académie Julian where he studied between 1889 and 1891. He exhibited at the 1890 Salon and received an Honorable Mention. He was also represented at the Paris Universal Exposition of 1900. He exhibited frequently at the N.A.D. in New York, receiving the Third Hallgarten Prize in 1888 and the Second in 1895. In 1896 he was awarded the First Hallgarten Prize, but this was subsequently withdrawn by the jury because he had passed the age of thirty-five. In 1901 he was assistant director of fine arts for the Pan-American Exposition in Buffalo. In 1904 he was made a full academician of the N.A.D. From this time on, he was active in Academy affairs, eventually becoming its corresponding secretary. About 1900 Curran began spending summers at the artists' colony of Cragsmoor, New York, and shortly became one of its leading members. Most of his landscape works, usually peopled by young ladies, were painted there. He was also active as a portrait painter for most of his career.

De Camp, Joseph Rodefer (1858-1923)

De Camp was born in Cincinnati, Ohio. He attended the McMicken School of Design at the University of Cincinnati, then taught drawing at a girls' school in Chillicothe, Ohio. Having heard of Frank Duveneck and wishing to study with him, he traveled to Munich where he enrolled at the Royal Academy in 1878. There he met William Merritt Chase, John Henry Twachtman, and Theodore Wendel (qq.v.), among others. Upon returning to America he went to New York, but by 1881 he was in Boston where he was impressed by the work of Edmund Charles Tarbell. From this time on he lived for the most part in Boston where he became a member of the Boston School and taught at the museum. In 1899 he won the Temple Gold Medal awarded by the Pennsylvania Academy of the Fine Arts; in 1900 he took an Honorable Mention at the Paris Universal Exposition. In 1903 he began to teach at the Massachusetts Normal School. In 1906 he was appointed instructor of painting at the Pennsylvania Academy. His first one-man show took place in 1911 at the St. Botolph Club in Boston. In 1922 he moved with his family to fashionable Beacon Hill. Although primarily a figure painter, especially of portraits and of pensive women in indoor settings, he also tried his hand at landscape. He died while on vacation in Florida.

Enneking, John Joseph (1838-1916)

Enneking was born in Minister, Ohio, of German parents who died when he was still young. In 1858 he entered Mount St. Mary's College in Cincinnati where he learned to draw. He never graduated. In 1861 he joined the Union Army and was severely wounded. In 1864 he went to New York, but quickly left. After a short painting trip to the Adirondacks, he made his way to Boston where he studied industrial drawing and worked as a tinsmith. In 1864 he married Mary Eliot, daughter of a wealthy merchant, and with money inherited from his uncle, they started a tinware manufactory. This failed, and subsequently, after some instruction from the landscape painter Samuel L. Gerry, Enneking began to paint landscapes. These sold well, and after three years he and his family traveled, between 1872 and 1876, through France, Italy, Switzerland, and Germany. In Paris, Enneking studied under Léon Bonnat and met Corot and Millet. He also befriended Monet and Daubigny, and his work became impressionistic. Back in Boston, he began a life of prolific productivity, exhibiting regularly at the St. Botolph Club, the Paint and Clay Club, and the Copley Society. In Boston he was a pioneer Impressionist who was generally held in high regard. His work always sold well.

Frieseke, Frederick Carl (1874-1939)

Frieseke was born in Owosso, Michigan. He studied briefly first at the Art Institute of Chicago and later at the Art Students' League in New York. At the age of twenty-four he went to Paris and stayed there the rest of his life. He studied at the Académie Julian and with Benjamin Constant and Jean-Paul Laurens. An Impressionist from the start, he exhibited in the Salons in the early 1900s and was made an associate of the Société Nationale des Beaux-Arts. In 1904, the same year in which one of his paintings was purchased for the Musée de Luxembourg, he won the Silver Medal at the St. Louis Universal Exposition and the Gold Medal at the Munich Exposition. In 1906, the year after his marriage, he rented a house in Giverny next to Monet's. In 1914 his daughter Frances, who became one of his favorite models, was born. In 1915 he won the Grand Prize for painting at the Panama-Pacific Exposition in San Francisco. From about this time until his death he exhibited continually and successfully both in America and Europe. He was made a chevalier of the Legion of Honor in 1920. He died in his home at Mesnil-sur-Blangy in Normandy. His pictures are usually of women in outdoor or, less frequently, indoor settings.

Goodwin, Arthur Clifton (1864-1929)

Goodwin was born in Portsmouth, New Hampshire, but grew up in Chelsea, Massachusetts. He worked in a wholesale paper establishment for a number of years and is said to have been so dissatisfied with his job that he took to heavy drinking. He began to paint about 1902 and was chiefly a self-taught artist. A good friend of the Boston painter Louis Kronberg, who encouraged him and in whose studio he frequently worked, Goodwin was welcomed in Boston School circles and quickly picked up an Impressionist-influenced style. His speciality was atmospheric scenes of Boston, but he also did a number of seascapes. Kronberg, who seems to have been a particular influence on him, encouraged him to master the pastel medium in which Goodwin became quite proficient. In 1921 he moved to New York where he rented a studio until 1923. That year he moved with his wife to a farm at Old Chatham, New York, where he lived in comparative seclusion until his return to Boston in late 1928 or early 1929. His friend Kronberg advised him at that time to go to Paris, but he died of excessive drinking on May 9, 1929, a steamship ticket to France in his packed trunk. Although Goodwin was not a well-known artist in his lifetime, his reputation has increased since the one-man retrospective held at the Wildenstein Gallery in New York in 1946. That exhibition was organized by the noted art historian Lionello Venturi.

Hassam, Frederick Childe (1859-1935)

Hassam, born in Dorchester, Massachusetts, of old New England stock, manifested an aptitude for drawing early in his life. By the age of nineteen he had become a competent wood engraver and had established himself as an illustrator, contributing to *Harper's*, *Scribner's*, and the *Century*. Beginning about 1879 he studied with Ignaz Marcel Gaugengigl, an established Boston painter. In 1883 he traveled to Holland, Spain, and Italy, and in 1884 he married Kathleen M. Doane. In 1886 he went on a second trip to Europe and this time stayed for three years. He studied at the Académie Julian in Paris and also worked independently in his own studio. He exhibited at the Paris Salon in 1887 and 1888 and in 1889 won a Bronze Medal at the Universal Exposition. After his return to America he settled in New York. His style was now closely related to Monet's though he often denied this. Hassam spent his summers in resorts favored by artists such as the Isles of Shoals, off the coast of New Hampshire; Old Lyme, Connecticut; and Gloucester, Massachusetts. Many of his landscapes depict these sites. In 1897 he resigned from the Society of American Artists and joined the Ten American Painters. In 1906 he beame a full member of the National Academy of Design. The first of many one-man shows was held at the Montross Gallery in New York in 1905. During his later years he was chiefly interested in printmaking.

Henri, Robert
(1865-1929)

Henri was born Robert Henry Cozad in Cincinnati, Ohio. In 1882 his father shot a man in self-defense, and other members of the family changed their names. In 1886 he went to Philadelphia where he studied at the Pennsylvania Academy of the Fine Arts under Thomas Anshutz. In 1888 he went to Paris and stayed there until 1891, studying at the Académie Julian. There he took an interest in Impressionism. After his return he studied with the Impressionist painter Robert Vonnoh (q.v.) in Philadelphia. In 1892 he began teaching at the Philadelphia School of Design for Women and began to meet regularly with John Sloan, William Glackens, George Luks, and Everett Shinn. He went to Europe again in 1895-96 and 1898-1900 and was influenced by the works of Manet, Velázquez, and Hals. When he returned, he settled in New York where he became the leader of the anti-establishment artists. He organized the exhibition of The Eight at the Macbeth Gallery in New York in 1908 which launched the Ash Can School. In 1910 he helped organize the Society of Independent Artists. Henri was the central figure among progressive American artists until the Armory Show of 1913.

Holmes, William Henry
(1846-1933)

Holmes was born near Cadiz, Ohio, and showed artistic promise as a youth. He attended normal schools in Ohio, but by 1866 he had decided to be an artist. About 1867-68 he applied to E.F. Andrews, in Steubenville, Ohio, for an apprenticeship, but the artist did not take students. He then attended the State Normal School in Salem, Massachusetts, where he was encouraged to study painting with Theodore Kauffman in Washington, D.C. He was soon hired as a natural science draftsman by the Smithsonian Institution, a position he left in 1872 to become an artist with the U.S. Geological Survey of the Territories. In 1875, as an assistant geologist with the Survey, he visited the cliff-dwellings of the Pueblo and became interested in Indian archaeology. Four years later, in 1879-1880, he traveled to Europe, studying in Munich, where he met Frank Duveneck and visiting Rome, Venice, and Naples. For four years after his return Holmes pursued a career as a research ethnologist and archaeologist at the Smithsonian Institution. In 1894 he was made head curator of the Field Museum of Natural History in Chicago. He returned to Washington, D.C. in 1897 to become head curator of the department of anthropology at the National Museum. After holding other posts, in 1920 he was made director of the National Gallery of Art (now the National Museum of American Art). Throughout his career he executed and exhibited watercolors.

Koeniger, Walter
(1881-1943)

Koeniger was born in Germany and received his early artistic training there. Not much is known about his life. His father, a successful architect and builder, wanted him to join the family business, but Koeniger refused. Probably to escape his family's censure, he came to America in 1911 or 1912. He joined the artists' colony at Woodstock, New York, and painted there for most of the rest of his life. He was a member of the Salmagundi Club but seems to have belonged to no other organizations. His specialty was winter landscapes painted in a sunset light.

Lawson, Ernest
(1873-1939)

Born in Halifax, Nova Scotia, Lawson went to New York at the age of eighteen to study at the Art Students' League. Previously he had studied at the Kansas City Art League School in 1888 and at the Academia de San Carlos in Mexico City in 1889. In New York he studied under J. Alden Weir and John Henry Twachtman (qq.v.), both Impressionists. In 1893 Lawson went to Paris where he enrolled at he Académie Julian but quickly left it in order to study on his own. During this visit he met Alfred Sisley and was encouraged by him. By 1894 he was back in New York and studying with Weir and Twachtman at their summer school in Cos Cob. He exhibited with The Eight in 1908 but was really not an avant-garde painter. His style was a bold impressionist one that effectively captured the sites around upper Manhattan where he lived in the early 1900s. During his career Lawson won many prizes and awards. In 1921 he was the Gold Medal winner at the Carnegie International in Pittsburgh.

Lever, Hayley
(1876-1958)

Lever was born in Adelaide, South Australia, and was educated there. In 1899 he went to England and, after studying and exhibiting in London and Paris, spent some years at the village of St. Ives in Cornwall. In 1911 he visited the United States and painted his first American scenes. These were very well received, and he decided to stay in this country. In 1914 he was given one-man shows at the Syracuse Museum of Fine Arts and at the Memorial Art Gallery in Rochester. In 1915 he was awarded the Gold Medal at the Panama-Pacific International Exposition. In 1917 he won the Sesnan Gold Medal at the Pennsylvania Academy of the Fine Arts. Between 1919 and 1931 he taught at the Art Students' League, New York. For the most part, he lived in New York, though he traveled in the summer to New England as well as to Long Island and New Jersey, in all of which he painted. In 1930 he moved to Caldwell, New Jersey, but retained his studio in New York City. In 1933 he was elected an academician of the National Academy of Design. In 1938 he moved to Mount Vernon, New York, where he died.

Metcalf, Willard Leroy
(1858-1925)

Metcalf was born in Lowell, Massachusetts, where he received his early education. At seventeen he was apprenticed to a wood engraver, and the following year he entered the studio of the Boston landscape painter George Loring Brown. During the years 1876 and 1877 he attended life classes at the Lowell Institute in Boston. Later, he also attended the Massachusetts Normal Art School and the School of the Museum of Fine Arts, both in Boston. In 1881 and 1882 he traveled to the Southwest, working as an illustrator, and in 1883 he went to Paris to study at the Académie Julian. He received an Honorable Mention in the Paris Salon of 1888. In 1887 he was at Giverny with Theodore Robinson (q.v.) and probably met Monet. He returned to Boston in 1889 but shortly thereafter moved to New York where he taught at the Art Students' League and at the Cooper Institute. He joined the Society of American Artists in 1887 but left it to become one of the Ten American Painters in 1898. In the following years he won many prizes and awards. About 1900 he established a summer studio at Chester, Vermont. In 1903 he left New York to paint in Maine, and from that time on he devoted himself to painting the New England landscape.

Miller, Richard Emil (1875-1943)

Miller was born in St. Louis, Missouri, where he received his early artistic training. In 1898 he went to Paris to study at the Académie Julian. He joined a number of American artists' associations in Paris and came under the influence of Frederick Carl Frieseke (q.v.). In 1904 he won a Second Medal at the Paris Salon, and about this time the French government began to purchase a number of his works. In 1908 he was made a chevalier of the Legion of Honor. He taught at the Atelier Colarossi in Paris and held summer classes in Giverny. In 1909 he had a small one-man show at the Venice Biennale. Though closely identified with Frieseke, his color was stronger and applied in patches. In 1906 he visited America, but returned to Paris. In 1918, at the end of World War I, he returned to the United States for good. He settled in Provincetown, Massachusetts, where he taught.

Paxton, William McGregor (1869-1941)

Born in Baltimore, Maryland, Paxton grew up outside of Boston. In 1887 he received a scholarship to study at the Cowles Art School in Boston under Dennis Miller Bunker (q.v.). In 1889 he went to Paris to study at the Ecole des Beaux-Arts under Bunker's teacher, Jean-Léon Gérôme; he also took classes at the Académie Julian. While in Paris the collection of the critic Thoré-Burger, with its several paintings by Jan Vermeer, was sold at auction, and Paxton was exposed to the work of the master he later sought to imitate. After returning to Boston in 1893 he again attended the Cowles Art School where he was influenced by Joseph Rodefer De Camp (q.v.). In 1904 he lost, as did De Camp, an enormous quantity of work in a studio fire. That same year he joined the faculty of the School of the Museum of Fine Arts, and from about this time on his scenes of women at leisure in luxurious interiors took on a highly finished Vermeeresque quality. In 1904 he won a Bronze Medal at the St. Louis Universal Exposition and in 1910 won the Popular Prize at the Pennsylvania Academy of the Fine Arts. In years following he won a number of such popular prizes at various institutions, an indication that his work held great appeal for the public at large.

Pearson, Marguerite Stuber (1898-1978)

Pearson was born in Philadelphia but received her artistic education in Boston at the School of the Museum of Fine Arts and from a number of Boston artists, most important among them Edmund C. Tarbell. Though a relative latecomer, she identified with the aims of the Boston School and was a prolific painter of interior genre scenes and still lifes. As a result of contracting poliomyelitis while a young adult, she was a paraplegic for virtually all of her working life. Pearson exhibited frequently at the Rockport Art Association, at the Ogunquit Art Association, and at the Grand Central Galleries in New York. She maintained a studio in Rockport, Massachusetts, where she died.

Potthast, Edward Henry (1857-1927)

Potthast was born in Cincinnati and received his early artistic education at the McMicken School of Design. Beginning at age seventeen he worked at a lithographer's establishment. This employment lasted for eight years, at the end of which he had saved enough money out of a small salary to finance a trip to Europe. Instead of going to Paris, as did most of his contemporaries, he went to Antwerp where he studied with Charles Vériat. Later he went to Munich. At the end of three years, Potthast returned to Cincinnati and resumed work as a lithographer. Between 1887 and 1889 he again went to Europe, this time to Germany and France, where he was particularly impressed by the Barbizon School. It was Robert Vonnoh (q.v.) who introduced him to Impressionism. Back in Cincinnati he devoted himself increasingly to painting, and in 1894 the Cincinnati Art Museum bought one of his works. In 1896 he moved to New York where he lived for the rest of his life. By 1908 he had settled in a studio at the Gainsborough building on Central Park South. A shy man who never married, Potthast nevertheless had many artist friends. He traveled a great deal, especially in the summer, to towns along the New England coast. From these sketching trips resulted the numerous beach scenes that are the hallmark of his career.

Prendergast, Maurice Brazil (1859-1924)

Born in St. John's, Newfoundland, Prendergast grew up in Boston where his family moved in 1861. Not much is known of his early years, but he did work for a commercial art firm and by 1883 was earning his living as an illustrator. In 1886 he and his brother Charles, his constant companion, made their way to England on a cattle boat; they may also have been to Paris. They returned to America the following year and, over the next four years, both worked to save the money needed to send Maurice to Paris. By 1891, Maurice had arrived there; he studied first at the Atelier Colarossi, then at the Académie Julian. He befriended a Canadian painter, James Wilson Morrice, and he was introduced to Walter Sickert and Aubrey Beardsley. Under Morrice's influence Prendergast developed an interest in figure painting and in urban scenes of people in leisure activities. The works of the Postimpressionists Pierre Bonnard and Edouard Vuillard particularly influenced him. Back in the Boston area in 1894 or 1895 Prendergast soon joined his brother at nearby Winchester. He went on sketching trips to beach towns around Boston and produced paintings and watercolors of scenes observed there. After the exhibition of his work at the Boston Water Color Club in 1897, Prendergast commanded increasing patronage. In 1898 and 1899 he spent eighteen months in Europe, principally in Venice. He returned to live in Boston again but exhibited his work in other cities as well and made many trips to New York and Europe. In 1908 he exhibited with The Eight at the Macbeth Gallery in New York; in 1914 he and his brother moved there. After this time he worked in New York during the winter and sketched in New England during the summer.

Redfield, Edward Willis (1869-1965)

Redfield was born in Bridgeville, Delaware, but moved to Philadelphia as a young boy. After completing studies at the Pennsylvania Academy of the Fine Arts he went to Paris where he studied at the Académie Julian. His teachers there were William-Adolphe Bouguereau and Tony Robert-Fleury, and he had a work exhibited in the 1890 Salon. He returned to America and painted with varying success. In 1889 he went back for a brief trip to Fontainebleau, which he especially liked, and it was during this trip that he met his wife, whom he married in London in 1893. Redfield bought a farmhouse in Bucks County, Pennsylvania, shortly after his second trip to Europe; eventually he moved there with his family. In 1900 he won the Bronze Medal at the Paris Exposition. In 1904 he received the Second Hallgarten Prize at the National Academy of Design and in 1907 the Gold Medal of Honor of the Pennsylvania Academy. He exhibited often at the Carnegie Internationals in Pittsburgh and in 1914 won the Gold Medal. He mostly painted in the open in the vicinity of his house and for forty years specialized in autumn and winter landscapes of the Pennsylvania countryside.

Reid, Robert Lewis
(1862-1929)

Reid was born in Stockbridge, Massachusetts. In 1880 he entered the School of the Museum of Fine Arts, Boston, where he studied under Otto Grundmann. He quickly progressed and was made an assistant instructor as well as editor of the school's publication. Among his fellow students and close friends there were Willard L. Metcalf (q.v.) and Edmund C. Tarbell. In 1885 he went to Paris to study at the Académie Julian. He did not embrace Impressionism but rather attempted to paint in the style of Jules Bastien-Lepage. After his return to America in 1889 he settled in New York and concentrated on painting murals. His easel paintings, however, became progressively more impressionist in style. From 1893 to 1896 he taught at the Art Students' League. In 1897 he joined the Ten American Painters; the following year he received the Hallgarten Prize awarded by the National Academy of Design. Until 1917, when he moved to Colorado Springs and became chiefly a portrait painter, he was mostly engaged with mural commissions. His last years were spent in poor health; after a stroke paralyzed his right side in 1927 he taught himself to paint with his left hand.

Ritman, Louis
(1889-1963)

Ritman was born in Russia but arrived in the United States with his parents in 1903. The family settled in Chicago, and it was there that he received his early training under Wellington J. Reynolds. In 1909 he studied briefly with William Merritt Chase (q.v.) in Philadelphia before going to Europe. Between 1909 and 1914 he was at the Ecole des Beaux-Arts in Paris. By 1911, influenced by numerous trips to Giverny where he eventually rented a house, he had become a full-fledged Impressionist. Back in Chicago in 1915, he participated in a number of exhibitions, and at this time the city purchased one of his works. Ritman returned to France in 1916 and stayed there until 1919. He returned to Chicago once more and in 1922 was awarded the Hallgarten Prize by the National Academy of Design in New York. From this time on Ritman exhibited frequently and successfully at the Carnegie Internationals, at the Pennsylvania Academy of the Fine Arts, and at the Art Institute of Chicago. In 1931 and again in 1939 he made painting trips to France. In 1950 he was elected an academician of the N.A.D. Between 1951 and 1963 he spent summers in southeastern Michigan where he painted many landscapes.

Robinson, Theodore
(1852-1896)

Robinson was born in Irasburg, Vermont, the son of a Methodist minister, but he grew up in Evansville, Wisconsin. He studied art for a brief period in Chicago in 1869 or 1870. In 1874 he went to New York where he took classes at the National Academy of Design and helped found the Art Students' League. In 1876 he went to France, and after traveling in Normandy he took a studio in Paris. There he studied chiefly under Jean-Léon Gérôme at the Ecole des Beaux-Arts. After further travel and meeting James McNeill Whistler in Venice, he returned to America in 1879, settling in New York two years later. He supported himself at this time by teaching and painting architectural decorations. In 1884 he returned to France, and in 1888 he met Claude Monet at Giverny. He became an Impressionist, and in 1892 he returned to America with the purpose of painting native landscapes in this style. Though he was not successful financially he nevertheless had an enormous influence on fellow artists. In 1895 his first one-man show was held at the Macbeth Gallery in New York and later traveled to other cities. Never a healthy individual, he died at the age of forty-four of asthma.

Russell, Walter
(1871-1963)

Born in Boston, Russell was one of the truly picturesque figures in American art. His family was poor, and as a youth Russell lived by his wits. He had no formal schooling, save for a stint in art school at about the age of fifteen, but he possessed great artistic and musical talent. About 1895 he went abroad to study and enrolled at the Académie Julian though he studied largely on his own. After his return home in 1897 he settled in New York and became an art editor at *Collier's*, becoming an artist and correspondent for the magazine during the Spanish-American War. Between 1901 and 1904 he specialized in portraits of children and wrote and illustrated a number of children's books. In 1900 his allegorical work *The Might of Ages* won a Special Mention at the Turin International Exposition in Italy. Although at this time he supported himself primarily from his artistic endeavors, Russell was always trying out new ideas and devising schemes to implement them. One of his controversial ideas, cooperative housing, had a huge success, and Russell built the Hôtel des Artistes as well as other innovative buildings in New York. About 1927 Russell abandoned painting and took up sculpture. He fashioned busts of Theodore Roosevelt, Franklin D. Roosevelt, and Thomas Edison, but his greatest achievement was probably the Mark Twain Memorial in Hannibal, Missouri. About this time he began to develop scientific theories that ran against Newtonian and Keplerian physics, and Russell gained a reputation as an eccentric. He persisted in his views, however, and in 1949 founded the University of Science and Philosophy, a positive-thinking correspondence school he ran from his estate in the Blue Ridge Mountains in Virginia.

Sargent, John Singer
(1856-1925)

Sargent was born in Florence of American parents. He was truly an expatriate, but he always retained his American citizenship and loved to associate with American artists. His early training was in Italy, but in 1874 he entered the atelier of Emile-Auguste Carolus-Duran in Paris. With the encouragement of his teacher he developed a brilliant technique designed to capture fleeting impressions through quick brushwork. His visits to Spain and Holland in 1879 and 1880, where he saw and admired works by Hals and Velázquez, also helped shape his style. A great success in Paris, Sargent worked there until 1886 when he moved to London largely as the result of the scandal caused by his *Madame X* (Metropolitan Museum of Art, New York) at the 1884 Salon. In England he became *the* painter of the wealthy and fashionable. He made many trips to America beginning in 1876, and by 1890 he was working on murals for the Boston Public Library. In 1897 he was made an academician of the National Academy of Design in New York, a member of the Royal Academy in London, and an officer of the Legion of Honor in France, honors that reflected his international reputation. After about 1909 he grew dissatisfied with portraiture, and he became increasingly interested in watercolor painting. During World War I he painted many of these showing battlefield scenes with British troops. He died in London.

Schofield, Walter Elmer
(1867-1944)

Schofield was born in Philadelphia. About 1885 he attended Swarthmore College but never graduated. After a trip to Texas in 1886-87 he began serious artistic studies at the Pennsylvania Academy of the Fine Arts under Thomas Anshutz. From about 1890 to 1895 he was in Paris studying at the Ecole des Beaux-Arts, at the Académie Julian, and under various teachers. He was probably back in the United States about 1900, but it is certain that from 1902 until his death he spent most of his time abroad. He particularly liked Brittany and Normandy in France and Devon and Cornwall in England. After serving in the British army during World War I he established his studio in Cornwall. Schofield exhibited often in America and kept up his American connections. In the public mind he was associated with Edward Willis Redfield (q.v.) and with Daniel Garber as a member of a Pennsylvania school of artists, but, more often than not, his usually large-sized landscapes had been painted abroad. In 1904 he received the Gold Medal at the Carnegie International in Pittsburgh. He died in Cornwall.

Simmons, Edward Emerson (1852-1931)

Simmons was born in Concord, Massachusetts, and attended Harvard College, graduating in 1874. After attempting to make a living at various occupations in several cities, by 1877 he was back in Boston, determined to become an artist. He studied under William Rimmer and enrolled at the School of the Musem of Fine Arts, but, due to disagreements with his teachers, decided to study abroad. In 1878 he left for Paris where he studied at the Académie Julian for a number of years. In 1881 the academy awarded him a prize for drawing, and in 1882 he won an Honorable Mention at the Paris Salon. Between 1881 and 1886 Simmons lived and worked at Concarneau on the coast of Brittany, visiting Elche, Spain, for months at a time. In 1887 he moved to St. Ives in Cornwall, bringing with him his wife and son. Here he worked with Theodore Robinson (q.v.) for about five years and spent summers in various parts of Europe. In 1891 he returned to America and, after working on the decorations for the dome of the Manufactures Building at the World's Columbian Exposition in Chicago, decided to devote his energies to mural painting. After a great success with murals which he executed at the New York City Criminal Court in 1893 he seldom lacked commissions. In 1898 he joined the Ten American Painters though he exhibited few works with them. In 1914 he was one of the three artists commissioned to decorate the buildings of the Panama-Pacific Exposition in San Francisco. He died in Baltimore, Maryland.

Symons, George Gardner (1861?-1930)

Gardner Symons was born in Chicago of German parents. His original surname was Simon. He is believed to have studied at the Art Institute of Chicago, but this is not certain. Later he studied in Paris, Munich, and London for about ten years. In 1896 he was in America and visited California in the company of the landscape painter William Wendt. In 1899 he exhibited at the Royal Academy in London, and at about this time he probably began to work in the village of St. Ives in Cornwall. There he met Walter Elmer Schofield (q.v.), and their styles developed in a more or less similar manner. By 1906 he was back in America. Between 1906 and 1915 he worked at Laguna Beach, California, but he also spent much time on the East Coast. He had a house in Colerain, Massachusetts, and it is there that he painted most of the winter scenes for which he gained a reputation. In 1909 he won the Carnegie Prize at the National Academy of Design in New York, and in 1911 he became a full academician there. Between 1910 and 1922 he exhibited frequently and successfully. His landscapes were usually associated with those of Schofield and Edward Redfield (q.v.). He died in Hillside, New Jersey.

Twachtman, John Henry (1853-1902)

Twachtman was born in Cincinnati, Ohio, of German parents. In 1868 he enrolled in the evening drawing class at the Ohio Mechanics Institute; three years later he went to the McMicken School of Design. In 1875 Frank Duveneck, a family friend as well as his teacher, invited him to work in the studio he shared with Henry Farny. When Duveneck returned to Munich in 1875, Twachtman went with him to study at the Royal Academy. In 1877 he spent about nine months in Venice with Duveneck and William Merritt Chase (q.v.); the following year he returned to America, eventually settling in New York. There he joined the Society of American Artists in 1880 and the Tile Club. After his marriage in 1887 he went to England, Holland, Belgium, and Germany. In Holland he painted with J. Alden Weir (q.v.), who was a life-long friend, and came to admire the works of Anton Mauve. In 1883 he decided to continue his studies in Paris for two years, enrolling in the Académie Julian where he met the many Americans studying there. His style dramatically changed at this time. After his return to America he worked in Chicago and New York. In 1888 he won the Webb Prize awarded by the Society of American Artists. The following year he commenced his long teaching career at the Art Students' League. That same year he purchased a house at Cos Cob near Greenwich, Connecticut, and from this time on he devoted himself to painting landscapes of scenes in and around his property. In 1897 he helped found the Ten American Painters. After 1900 he spent his summers in Gloucester, Massachusetts. He died suddenly at an early age.

Vonnoh, Robert William
(1858-1933)

The son of an immigrant German cabinetmaker, Vonnoh was born in Hartford, Connecticut, but he grew up in Boston. At fourteen he went to work for a lithographic firm and began to take classes in the evening. In 1875 he enrolled in the Massachusetts Normal Art School where he studied under Edward R. Smith. In 1881 he went to Paris to study at the Académie Julian, where he spent two years under Jules-Joseph Lefebvre and Gustave Boulanger. In 1887 he returned to France, painting mostly portraits and landscapes executed outdoors in an impressionist style. After four years he returned to America and became an advocate of the new style. He taught at the Cowles Art School in Boston in 1884 and 1885 and at the School of the Museum of Fine Arts from 1885 to 1887. From 1891 to 1896 he taught figure painting at the Pennsylvania Academy of the Fine Arts and influenced such younger artists as Edward Redfield, Robert Henri (qq.v.), and John Sloan. In 1892 he joined the Society of American Artists. He had studios in New York and Chicago about 1900 and frequently painted at Old Lyme, Connecticut, during the summer. About 1910 he began frequent visits to Grez-sur-Loing, France, to paint. After 1918 he again taught at the Pennsylvania Academy. He spent his last years in France suffering from badly deteriorated eyesight.

Weir, Julian Alden
(1852-1919)

The son of the artist Robert W. Weir, J. Alden Weir was born at West Point, New York, where his father was professor of drawing at the U.S. Military Academy. In 1873 he went to Paris where he studied at the Ecole des Beaux-Arts under Jean-Léon Gérôme. He also traveled to Holland and Spain, returning to New York in 1877. Initially horrified by Impressionism he remained an admirer of the style of Jules Bastien-Lepage until about 1890. He was a charter member of the Society of American Artists and exhibited frequently at the National Academy of Design. In 1880, 1881, and 1883 he traveled to Europe to buy paintings for an American collector; works by Manet and Bastien-Lepage were among his purchases. In 1886 he became an academician of the National Academy. In 1889 he and his close friend John Henry Twachtman (q.v.) held a highly successful joint exhibition at the Ortgies Gallery in New York. In the 1890s his style began to change, and in 1891 the works at his one-man show at the Blakeslee Gallery displayed the influence of Impressionism. In 1897 he joined the Ten American Painters. As an impressionist his works gained wide acclaim as well as numerous medals and prizes. From 1915 to 1917 he was president of the National Academy. His summer home in Branchville, Connecticut, was a favorite retreat, and he painted many landscapes there.

Wendel, Theodore
(1859-1932)

Born in Midway, Ohio, Wendel first studied art at the Cincinnati School of Design. In 1878 he traveled to Europe and, as did so many young Midwestern artists, studied at the Royal Academy in Munich. In 1879 he joined Frank Duveneck's class at Polling, Germany, and between 1879 and 1881 visited Florence and Venice with Duveneck's group. He returned to America, probably in 1881. Two years later he shared a studio with Kenyon Cox in Newport, Rhode Island. Around 1885 or 1886 Wendel returned to Europe and studied briefly at the Académie Julian in Paris. In 1886-87 he spent the summers at Giverny, where he met Monet. At this time he produced his first impressionist paintings. In 1889 he returned to the United States and, with the possible exception of a trip to Europe in 1890-91, stayed there until 1897. From 1892 he lived in Boston where he taught at the Cowles Art School and at Wellesley College. After his marriage in 1897 he visited France and Italy for two years. He lived at Ipswich, Massachusetts after 1899, staying there for the rest of his life and painting many scenes of the town and its surrounding countryside. In 1915 he won the Silver Medal at the Panama-Pacific International Exposition in San Francisco and was given a one-man show at the Guild of Boston Artists. After an illness in 1917 he painted infrequently.

Whorf, John
(1903-1959)

Whorf was born in Boston. His father, a commercial artist, began to instruct him in art at the age of fourteen. He first studied at the School of the Museum of Fine Arts in Boston but later traveled in France and Spain. In France he studied at the Atelier Colarossi; in Spain he received lessons from John Singer Sargent (q.v.). Although he was trained as an oil painter his real love was watercolor, and he turned to that medium early in his career. He achieved considerable fame as a watercolorist and exhibited annually in Boston and New York from about 1925 until his death. In 1938 he was awarded an honorary degree from Harvard University for his accomplishments in this medium. He died in Provincetown, Massachusetts, where he made his home for most of his adult life.

Bibliography

Books and Articles

Adams, Adeline, *Childe Hassam* (1938).

Ball, Robert, and Max W. Gottschalk, *Richard E. Miller, N.A.: An Impression and Appreciation* (1968).

Baur, John I. H., "Introducing Theodore Wendel," *Art in America* 64 (November-December 1976), pp. 102-112.

Baur, John I. H., "Photographic Studies by an Impressionist," *Gazette des Beaux-Arts*, ser. 6, 30 (October-November 1946), pp. 319-30.

Bellows, Emma S., *The Paintings of George Bellows* (1929).

Berry, Rose V. S., "Joseph De Camp: Painter and Man," *American Magazine of Art* 14 (April 1923), pp. 182-189.

Boyle, Richard J., *American Impressionism* (1974).

Boyle, Richard J., *John Twachtman* (1979).

Breeskin, Adelyn D., *Mary Cassatt: A Catalogue Raisonné of the Oils, Pastels, Water-Colors, and Drawings* (1970).

Brinton, Christian, *Impressions of the Art at the Panama-Pacific Exposition* (1916).

Brinton, Christian, "Robert Reid, Decorative Impressionist," *Arts & Decoration* 2 (November 1911), pp. 13-15, 34.

Buff, Barbara, "Cragsmoor, an Early American Art Colony," *Antiques* 114 (November 1978), pp. 1056-1067.

Charteris, Evan, *John Sargent* (1927).

Clark, Eliot, "The Art of Robert Vonnoh," *Art in America* 16 (August 1928), pp. 223-232.

Closson, William Baxter, "The Art of John J. Enneking," *International Studio* 76 (October 1922), pp. 3-6.

Cortissoz, Royal, *American Artists* (1923).

Davol, Ralph, "The Work of John J. Enneking," *American Magazine of Art* 8 (June 1917), pp. 320-325.

Downes, William Howe, "Boston Art and Artists," in F. Hopkinson Smith et al., *Essays on Art and Artists* (1896), pp. 265-280.

Downes, William Howe, "Joseph De Camp and His Work," *Art and Progress* 4 (April 1913), pp. 918-925.

Downes, William Howe, "William Merritt Chase, A Typical American Artist," *International Studio* 39 (December 1909), pp. xxxi-xxxvi.

Dreiser, Theodore, "C. C. Curran," *Truth* 18 (September 1899), pp. 227-230.

Du Bois, Guy Pène, "The Pennsylvania Group of Landscape Painters," *Arts & Decoration* 5 (July 1915), pp. 351-354.

Folk, Thomas, "Edward Redfield: Pennsylvania Impressionist," *Art and Antiques* 4 (March-April 1981), pp. 56-63.

Gammell, R. H. Ives, *Dennis Miller Bunker* (1953).

Garland, Hamlin, *Crumbling Idols: 12 Essays on Art* (1894).

Hale, Philip Leslie, "William McGregor Paxton," *International Studio* 39 (December 1909), pp. xlvi-xlviii.

Henri, Robert, *The Art Spirit* (1923, reprint ed. 1951).

Hind, C. Lewis, "An American Landscape Painter, W. Elmer Schofield," *International Studio* 48 (February 1913), pp. 280-289.

Hoeber, Arthur, "Edward Emerson Simmons," *Brush and Pencil* 5 (March 1900), pp. 241-249.

Hoopes, Donelson F., *Childe Hassam* (1979).

Hoopes, Donelson F., *The American Impressionists* (1972).

Huth, Hans, "Impressionism Comes to America," *Gazette des Beaux-Arts*, ser. 6, 29 (April 1946), pp. 225-252.

Laurvik, John Nilsen, "Edward Redfield," *International Studio* 41 (August 1910), pp. xxix-xxxvi.

Love, Richard H., *The Paintings of Louis Ritman (1889-1963)* (1975).

MacChesney, Clara, "Frederick Carl Frieseke – His Work and Suggestions for Painting from Nature," *Arts & Decoration* 3 (November 1912), pp. 13-15.

MacChesney, Clara, "Mary Cassatt and Her Work," *Arts & Decoration* 3 (June 1913), pp. 265-267.

McKibbin, David, *Sargent's Boston* (1956).

Mellerio, André, "Mary Cassatt," *L'Art et les Artistes* 12 (November 1919), pp. 69-75.

Milliken, William Matthewson, "Maurice Prendergast, American Artist," *The Arts* 9 (April 1926), pp. 181-192.

Mount, Charles Merrill, *John Singer Sargent: A Biography* (1957).

Muller, G. Frank, "Koeniger – Painter of Snow," *International Studio* 81 (June 1925), pp. 210-215.

Ormond, Richard, *John Singer Sargent* (1970).

Parkhurst, Thomas Shrewsbury, "Gardner Symons – Painter and Philosopher," *The Fine Arts Journal* 34 (November 1916), pp. 556-565.

Phillips, Duncan, *A Collection in the Making* (1926).

Pierce, Patricia Jobe, *The Ten* (1976).

Pisano, Ronald G., *William Merritt Chase* (1979).

Pousette-Dart, Nathaniel, *Childe Hassam* (1922).

Rewald, John, *Postimpressionism from Van Gogh to Gauguin* (1956).

Rewald, John, *The History of Impressionism* (1962).

Richardson, Edgar P., *Painting in America: The Story of 450 Years* (1956).

Roof, Katherine Metcalf, *The Life and Art of William Merritt Chase* (1917).

Ségard, Achille, *Un Peintre des Enfants et des Mères – Mary Cassatt* (1913).

Simmons, Edward, *From Seven to Seventy: Memories of a Painter and a Yankee* (1922).

Taylor, E. A., "The Paintings of F. C. Frieseke," *International Studio* 53 (October 1914), pp. 259-267.

Teevan, Bernard, "A Painter's Renaissance," *International Studio* 82 (October 1925), pp. 3-11.

Valerio, Edith, *Mary Cassatt* (1930).

Young, Dorothy Weir, *The Life and Letters of J. Alden Weir* (1960).

Exhibition Catalogues

Anderson, Dennis R., *Ernest Lawson*, ACA Galleries, New York, 1976.

Baur, John I. H.,*Theodore Robinson, 1852-1896*, The Brooklyn Museum, Brooklyn, 1946.

Cleveland Museum of Art, *Maurice Prendergast Memorial Exhibition*, 1926.

Coffin, William A., *Memorial Exhibition of the Works of Julian Alden Weir*, The Metropolitan Museum of Art, New York, 1924.

Domit, Moussa M., *Frederick Frieseke, 1874-1939*, Telfair Academy of Arts and Sciences, Savannah, Georgia, 1974.

Emerson, Sandra, Lucretia H. Giese, and Laura C. Luckey, *A. C. Goodwin, 1864-1929*, Museum of Fine Arts, Boston, 1974.

Gammell, R. H. Ives, *William McGregor Paxton, N.A., 1869-1941*, Indianapolis Museum of Art, Indianapolis, Indiana, 1978.

Gerdts, William H., *American Impressionism*, The Henry Art Gallery, University of Washington, Seattle, Washington, 1980.

Jacobowitz, Arlene, *Edward Henry Potthast, 1857 to 1927*, Chapellier Galleries, New York, 1969.

Johnston, Sona, *Theodore Robinson, 1852-1896*, The Baltimore Museum of Art, 1973.

Pach, Walter, *Maurice Prendergast Memorial Exhibition*, Whitney Museum of American Art, New York, 1931.

Pilgrim, Dianne H., *American Impressionist and Realist Paintings and Drawings, from the Collection of Mr. and Mrs. Raymond J. Horowitz*, The Metropolitan Museum of Art, New York, 1973.

Charles E. Slatkin Galleries, *Claude Monet and the Giverny Artists*, New York, 1960.

Venturi, Lionello, *Arthur Clifton Goodwin: A Selective Exhibition*, Addison Gallery of American Art, Phillips Academy, Andover, Massachusetts, 1946.